T0053727

The

BOOK OF
KILLER
PLANTS

THE BOOK OF KILLER PLANTS

Copyright © 2022 by Cider Mill Press Book Publishers LLC.

This is an officially licensed book by Cider Mill Press Book Publishers LLC.
All rights reserved under the Pan-American and International Copyright Conventions.

No part of this book may be reproduced in whole or in part, scanned, photocopied, recorded, distributed in any printed or electronic form, or reproduced in any manner whatsoever, or by any information storage and retrieval system now known or hereafter invented, without express written permission of the publisher, except in the case of brief quotations embodied in critical articles and reviews.

The scanning, uploading, and distribution of this book via the internet or via any other means without permission of the publisher is illegal and punishable by law. Please support authors' rights, and do not participate in or encourage piracy of copyrighted materials.

13-Digit ISBN: 978-1-64643-269-1
10-Digit ISBN: 1-64643-269-X

This book may be ordered by mail from the publisher. Please include $5.99 for postage and handling. Please support your local bookseller first!

Books published by Cider Mill Press Book Publishers are available at special discounts for bulk purchases in the United States by corporations, institutions, and other organizations. For more information, please contact the publisher.

Cider Mill Press Book Publishers
"Where good books are ready for press"
501 Nelson Place
Nashville, Tennessee 37214

cidermillpress.com

Typography: Calder, Warnock Pro

Printed in Malaysia

All vectors used under official license from Shutterstock.com.

23 24 25 26 27 OFF 6 5 4 3 2

The BOOK OF KILLER PLANTS

A Field Guide to
NATURE'S DEADLIEST CREATIONS

Kit Carlson, PhD

ILLUSTRATIONS BY EMILY SULLIVAN

CIDER MILL PRESS

BOOK PUBLISHERS

INTRODUCTION

"At first, there was an extraordinary almost pyrotechnic display of blue objects in all sizes and tints; as one became interested in the spots, a heavy weight was lowered on the top of the head and remained there while sharp pains shot through the temples...

On attempt to talk, wrong names were given to objects; although at the same time, the mind knew mistakes were made in speech, the words seemed to utter themselves independently."

—Alice E. Bacon, early American botanist

Excerpt from March 1903 *Rhodora: Journal of the New England Botanical Club.*

Documenting her results of self-experimentation with Baneberry ingestion.

Most people find the topic of plants and the toxins they produce inherently intriguing. Perhaps this is a consequence of humanity's perpetual challenge to determine which plants are edible, how to avoid or detoxify poisonous plants, and how to pass this knowledge on to future generations. Some folks have boldly committed themselves to the cause of understanding plant toxins through self-experimentation and sharing their experience with others. While we might have assumed this was the discovery process that only the earliest scientists used hundreds of thousands of years ago, humans have continued to use themselves as test subjects throughout history. The 19th- and 20th- century scientists were notably adventurous about self-experimentation with toxic substances. In her work, botanist Alice E. Bacon reported that she experienced a rapid heartbeat, throat constriction, intense abdominal and kidney pains, dizziness, and other disturbances after consuming Baneberry, scientifically known as *Actaea*. She concluded that she had firmly established *Actaea* to be poisonous, affecting the brain and circulatory system. She estimated a dozen berries would be a lethal dose. Although her methods were arguably dodgy, not to mention extremely unsafe, her conclusions were surprisingly accurate. Her published account can be fully appreciated in the March 1903 *Rhodora: Journal of the New England Botanical Club.*

So why are so many plants poisonous, and what makes them deadly? Unlike organisms that can run, swim, or fly away from predators, plants and fungi are sessile—fixed in place. They have leveraged immobility to maximize access to food and habitat without expending the energy required for movement. The cost of immobility is the constant pressure to defend their position and resources and avoid predation. Plants and fungi have become masterful chemists and have evolved the ability to synthesize a wide range of chemicals designed to deter, repel, manipulate, and even kill their predators.

PLANT DEFENSE STRATEGIES

A fundamental aspect of understanding plant toxins is considering why and how plants have evolved to produce toxins in the first place. In any ecosystem in the world, a complex web of interactions occurs between the species present. These interactions all revolve around the basic needs of every organism to survive and thrive. Many of these interactions are mutually beneficial; for instance, the berries of a tree provide food to birds, which then disperse the seeds in their excrement. Other interactions are detrimental to one or all organisms involved in the complex web of exchanges. The predator and prey relationship is arguably the most fundamental of interactions between organisms, where the predator kills prey for food. Plants are the prey in most of these relationships. They are locked in a perpetual battle to survive, evolving a myriad of adaptations to gain an advantage in this ageless conflict.

Just about everything attempts to feed on plants, including viruses, bacteria, fungi, nematodes, insects, and all vertebrates. Plants have evolved complex defense mechanisms and sophisticated communication strategies in response to the constant pressure of predation. These defenses may be always present in the plant, called constitutive defenses, or they may be activated by a variety of different triggers, called induced defenses.

CONSTITUTIVE DEFENSES
If you have ever walked through a patch of stinging nettles while wearing shorts, then you have experienced firsthand the effectiveness of a constitutive defense mechanism. Nettles are covered with stiff hairs called trichomes that have silica tips designed to break off and act like a syringe when the plant is disturbed, exposing the passerby to a cocktail of histamine, formic acid, and

serotonin. Any preformed and existing feature or chemical that functions for defense is considered a constitutive defense mechanism. These may include mechanical and structural defenses, indirect defenses, apparency defenses, and some forms of chemical defense.

MECHANICAL/STRUCTURAL DEFENSES

Mechanical and structural defenses are part of the plant's overall form and deter predation or make predation more difficult. The most basic example of this is the plant cell itself. Unlike animal cells, plant cells have cell walls that make them rigid, providing structure to the plant and forming a somewhat impenetrable barrier to invading microbes. Plants also have a waxy layer, called the cuticle, that covers plant stems and leaves and regulates the water content inside the plant, while also preventing microbes from making direct contact with plant cells. Due to its water-repelling properties, the cuticle also prevents water from collecting on stems and leaves, thereby reducing the ability of many pathogens to cause infection, because most pathogens require water to grow. The bark layer present on some plants is another structural defense. The outer bark is a water-resistant, protective layer of dead cells that prevents many potential predators from reaching the plant's living tissues.

The most well-recognized structural defenses are thorns, spines, and prickles. These structures have mainly evolved to deter vertebrate herbivory. For example, the Honey Locust tree, *Gleditsia triacanthos*, is densely covered with thousands of thick, long, viciously sharp spikes, so strong that they frequently cause flat tires on farm equipment. These spikes make the Honey Locust tree virtually impenetrable to all but the most persistent of larger herbivores.

Plants may also employ trichomes, specialized cells in the outer layer of plant tissues that grow into a hairlike structure. Trichomes on soybeans, for example, prevent insect eggs from being laid directly on the plant tissue, thus starving the larvae when the egg hatches. Some plants have trichomes that impale caterpillars moving across the leaf surface. Other plants have glandular hairs, specialized trichomes that repel insects and inhibit microbes by secreting toxic oils and acids.

INDIRECT DEFENSES

Indirect plant defenses are those traits that do not directly impact a predator's ability to attack the plant. Instead, they attract and manipulate other organisms that attack the plant's would-be predators. There are two basic constitutive indirect defense strategies, with some plants employing more than one.

First, a plant can attract defenders by providing food sources that attract them. These usually involve the production of nectar outside of the flower (extrafloral nectaries) or through the growth of solid food bodies, which can be fruit-like appendages or nutrient-rich layers of tissue. Second, plants can provide shelter to defenders. These shelters (called domatia) protect their defenders from predators or detrimental environmental conditions. The domatia can be as simple as folds in the stems or leaves covered with trichomes, or more complex structures with internal chambers and elaborate entrances. The most common examples of these mutually beneficial relationships include ants sheltered by *Acacia* and mites harbored by various plant species. The production of food sources and the presence of domatia do not directly attract potential defenders but increase the likelihood of having a defender present.

APPARENCY DEFENSES

Apparency defenses are those strategies that plants have evolved to make them less attainable to would-be predators—in other words, an ecological mechanism of escape from predators. Apparency defenses can be spatial, temporal, or cryptic (camouflage). Spatial apparency defenses involve the plant growing so that it is difficult for a predator to access, such as a plant growing on a cliff or other type of inaccessible habitat, or only developing leaves above or below the reach of predators. Temporal apparency defenses involve the plant strategically deploying a defense strategy at a time of day or year when a predator is less active. For example, some legumes, including common Red Clover (*Trifolium pratense*), secrete toxins from their leaves into the morning dew to prevent the growth of fungal pathogens. These toxins can also be problematic for grazing animals and cause intestinal distress and photodermatitis referred to as "dew poisoning." Cryptic defenses are equivalent to what we would call camouflage—that is, a plant's appearance makes it difficult for a predator to see it or makes it look unappetizing. Examples include Stone plants (*Lithops*), which look remarkably like stones sitting on the ground, and Sticky Sand Verbena (*Abronia latifolia*), which exude a sticky coating on their leaves—the plants are then covered with sand, effectively camouflaging them in their desert habitat.

INDUCED DEFENSES

The other category of defense responses is produced after exposure to a trigger; these are called induced defenses. There is a variety of different types of triggers; the fresh scent of newly cut grass is a good example of a trigger for an induced defense response. When grass is cut by a lawnmower, a mixture of volatile compounds is released, resulting in the characteristic fresh-grass smell. One of the most important of these compounds is jasmonic acid, which acts as a chemical messenger to surrounding plants, inducing the production of a cascade of toxic defense chemicals in nearby plants and additionally attracting parasitic wasps that reduce insect populations.

Induced defenses almost always involve the deployment of chemical defenses, which is the focus of this book. Plants produce or accumulate these chemicals to actively deter or even kill their predators. The defense chemicals could be found and collected from the external environment or could be novel molecules uniquely produced by the plant.

Some plants have evolved means of accumulating nontoxic compounds from the environment and incorporating them into their defense strategy, with silica and calcium being the most used. When silica is incorporated into plant tissues, it forms rocklike phytoliths. These phytoliths actively damage the mouthparts of grazing invertebrates and vertebrates. Calcium can form calcium oxalate crystals in plant tissues, which can pierce and cut soft tissues, causing pain and swelling. Furthermore, both chemicals increase the chance of an animal developing kidney stones, making these plants less palatable to potential herbivores.

Secondary metabolites are chemicals manufactured by the plant; they are not essential to its metabolic processes, meaning the plant doesn't need them for growth and reproduction. Instead, they are involved in improving its chance of survival. These secondary metabolites can be characterized as belonging to one of four broad classes: terpenoids, alkaloids, phenolics, and proteins. The roles of some secondary metabolites are still unknown.

TERPENOIDS are the largest and most diverse group of secondary metabolites, with at least 40,000 different kinds identified. All terpenoids are derived from a 5-carbon compound called isoprene.

They represent about 60% of the natural products currently known and are responsible for many characteristic properties of plants, such as the color of pumpkins, the smell of lavender, and the taste of cinnamon. Other terpenoids that most people are familiar with are the insecticidal pyrethrin and cannabinoids found in marijuana. Many terpenoids have significant pharmacological properties, which has led to their use in traditional and modern medicines.

For example, many species of plants in the Mint Family produce the terpenoid menthol. It is toxic to insects and antimicrobial, and it even suppresses the growth of neighboring plants. Humans have used menthol's properties for many beneficial purposes. It is an analgesic (meaning it relieves pain), lowers blood pressure, creates a cooling sensation, and is used as a scent and flavor in various products. Despite all the ways we use menthol, it is still toxic to humans in large quantities; as little as 3.5 g of menthol could be a lethal dose.

As plant defense mechanisms, terpenoids can play a variety of roles. Many of them are antifungal, antibacterial, or insecticidal. Some are toxic to vertebrate predators. Some terpenoids mimic insect pheromones, disrupting their reproductive process or larval development.

ALKALOIDS are a large group of nitrogen-containing compounds derived from amino acids, almost all of which have a bitter taste. Alkaloids are produced by many different plants, fungi, and invertebrates, and even some vertebrates. At least 4,000 alkaloids have been identified. Alkaloids that may be familiar to most people include caffeine, cocaine, nicotine, morphine, histamine, strychnine, and ephedrine. Like terpenoids, many alkaloids have significant pharmacological properties and are used in traditional and modern medicines.

An excellent example is caffeine. At least 30 species of plants produce caffeine—which can be found in coffee, tea, yerba mate, and cocoa—as a defense mechanism due to its toxicity to insects and fungi. It also suppresses the growth of neighboring plants and helps attract pollinators to flowers. And while caffeine can be toxic to humans in large quantities (75–100 cups of coffee), at low doses it acts as a central nervous system stimulant, reducing fatigue and drowsiness, and has become the most widely consumed psychoactive compound in the world today.

Another class of nitrogen-containing secondary metabolites is cyanogenic glycosides. These are compounds that are not toxic by themselves; however, certain enzymes in plants or the digestive tracts of animals react with the glycoside, leading to the formation of cyanide. Over 2,500 plant species produce cyanogenic glycosides for defense, including apples, almonds, cherries, linseed, sorghum, cassava, and loquats.

PHENOLICS are the third large category of secondary metabolites produced by plants. These compounds have a ring of six carbon atoms as their molecular base. Phenolics include several defense-related compounds, including flavonoids, tannins, lignins, and furanocoumarins. Flavonoids are the largest group of phenolics, with over 5,000 known types. Flavonoids provide many services to plants, besides being used as a defense mechanism. They are responsible for the coloration seen in many flowers, help absorb harmful UV radiation, and are involved in many physiological processes. Tannins are water-soluble and stored in vacuoles. They can bind to proteins in saliva and enzymes in the digestive tract. Animals that consume high concentrations of tannins will have a compromised digestive system, leading to reduced health or even death. Lignins are a group of large, complex molecules used by plants for structural support, primarily in bark and wood. Lignins are undigestible, waterproof, and rigid, creating a physical barrier against potential pathogens and grazers. Furanocoumarins are produced by a variety of plants and are especially common in the carrot and citrus plant families. Many of them are toxic to fungi, insects, and mammals. They can enter the outer cells of organisms, such as the skin, and bind to DNA when exposed to UV radiation, causing cell death and inflammation. Furanocoumarins in grapefruits affect enzymes in our liver and intestines, which can activate or deactivate many drugs, which is why some medications have a warning not to take them with grapefruit.

PROTEINS are large molecules composed of amino acids. Unlike the categories previously discussed, proteins require a much more significant output of plant energy and resources to be produced, so defensive proteins are primarily synthesized in response to an attack. Plant defense proteins include defensins, lectins, amylase inhibitors, proteinase inhibitors, and enzymes. Defensins are small protein molecules that can inhibit the growth of bacteria and fungi and constrain digestive proteins in herbivores. Lectins bind to carbohydrates and cause many problems in insects and vertebrates, such as disrupting the digestive process, clumping blood cells, and inhibiting protein synthesis. Amylase inhibitors are common in the bean family and inhibit starch digestion. Proteinase inhibitors are produced after an herbivore begins feeding on the plant. They enter the herbivore's digestive tract and hamper digestive enzymes. Defensive enzymes are produced in response to microbial pathogens, compromising the integrity of the cell walls of bacteria and fungi.

Plants produce many compounds to defend themselves from microbes, insects, and vertebrate herbivores. While most of these compounds are meant to deter or reduce attacks, some of them can be lethal. As with any substance, the amount of a chemical you are exposed to (dosage) determines the effects it will have. Even drinking excessive water over a short period can have detrimental, if not deadly, effects on the human body. Many of the compounds produced by the fungi and plants you are about to read about have beneficial effects on the human body in small doses, but are deadly at higher doses. Over the history of humankind, and with trial and error, we have determined which fungi and plants are edible, and which ones are deadly, and at what dosage. For at least some of the deadly ones, we have also discovered that specific procedures can neutralize or eliminate the toxic compound, such as boiling or cooking.

Accidental poisonings are often due to misidentification and a limited background in plant toxins. Many poisonous species closely resemble nontoxic species, and inexperienced foragers can make mistakes. Misidentification is particularly common in the case of mushrooms, which can be highly variable in appearance and are still not fully understood on a taxonomic level. Identification of many species of fungi and plants depends on very subtle differences, often at the microscopic level, which may not be readily discernible to the untrained eye. This book is a descriptive synopsis of plants and fungi containing compounds that could kill a human being. Do not collect and consume wild plants or mushrooms unless you are absolutely 100% sure of the identification.

The plants and mushrooms found in this collection are listed alphabetically by scientific name (first plants, then mushrooms). At the top of each entry, you will find the scientific name, common name(s), etymology, and family of the specimen.

USEFUL TERMS

Acetylcholine – A chemical messenger (neurotransmitter) that, when blocked or dysregulated, may cause muscle paralysis, heartbeat irregularities, and other potentially serious health consequences.

Alkaloid – A class of chemical compounds that are basic and contain at least one nitrogen ring. They tend to have a biological effect on living cells and often have poisonous or medicinal properties.

Alternate – A type of leaf arrangement where one leaf is attached per node on alternating sides.

Annual – A plant that completes its life cycle in one growing season.

Anoxia – A condition in which no oxygen is accessible to the brain or body.

Anthers – The male reproductive structures on flowering plants. Anthers produce pollen.

Anticholinergic – A compound that blocks the action of the chemical messenger acetylcholine. The anticholinergic effect can result in heartbeat irregularities (usually an increased heart rate), dry mouth, cognitive impairment, sedation, and other potentially serious health consequences.

Aril – A fleshy covering found around some seeds. The Yew tree has seeds that are covered with a red aril.

Axil – On a plant stem, the axil is the angle between the upper plant stem and the leaf.

Berry – A type of fruit, produced from the ripened ovary of a flowering plant. Berries typically have a fleshy pericarp.

Biennial – A plant that completes its life cycle over two growing seasons.

Bioactive – A compound that has a physiological effect on living cells and tissues.

Bract – A modified leaf that is often showy and adds visual appeal to flowers. The red petals of the Poinsettia are bracts.

Bulb – An underground reproductive storage organ of some plants, notably found in lilies. Bulbs are primarily composed of fleshy modified leaves, a short stem, and roots.

Cap – Also called a pileus, the cap is the head of a mushroom that is often rounded on the top, and sometimes colorful. The reproductive spores of the mushroom are contained inside the cap.

Carcinogen – A compound that may disrupt either genetic information or cellular processes in such a manner that cell production exceeds cell death, resulting in uncontrolled cell division.

Cholinergic – A compound that releases or produces acetylcholine and similar chemical messengers. The cholinergic effect can cause heartbeat irregularities, salivation, tear production, urination, defecation, and other potentially serious health consequences.

Corm – An underground reproductive storage organ of some plants, notably crocuses. Corms are primarily composed of a short, thick stem covered with a few scaly leaves.

Cyanogenic – A compound that contains cyanide or has the ability to produce cyanide.

Deciduous – Plants, typically trees, that seasonally lose their leaves.

Dioecious – Plants that produce separate male and female plants.

Drupe – A fruit type distinguished by containing a seed covered by a hard, stony pit, surrounded by a fleshy outer layer. Cherries, plums, and almonds are all examples of drupes.

Elliptical – A leaf shape characterized by having an oval-shaped leaf, wider at the base and tapered near the top. The leaf tends to be about twice as long as it is wide.

Endophytes – Microorganisms, typically fungi, that live inside plant tissues and have a symbiotic interaction with the host plant.

Evergreen – A plant that remains green during the entire year.

Family – A hierarchical taxonomic rank of plants above genus.

Florets –A small flower that makes up part of a larger flower arrangement (inflorescence) on a stem.

Follicle – A type of fruit that is dry at maturity and opens only on one side to release seeds.

Genus – A hierarchical taxonomic rank of plants above species.

Gills – Structures contained under the caps of mushrooms that hold sexual reproductive spores.

Glycosides – A class of chemical compounds that are characterized by having sugar molecules bound to other molecules with a glycosidic bound. There are a variety of different glycosides produced by plants that have a biological effect on living cells and often have poisonous or medicinal properties.

Habit – A tendency for a plant to have a particular growth form.

Hardiness zones – Defined growing areas with predictable climatic conditions, mostly including the warmest and coldest temperatures historically observed in a location.

Hemolytic – Involving the destruction of red blood cells.

Herbaceous – A plant that does not produce woody tissues.

Inflorescence – The arrangement of the flowers on a plant. The inflorescence can be an important identification characteristic.

Invasive – An organism that has been introduced into a new area and develops in any manner that is disruptive to the survival of the existing species.

Lanceolate – A leaf shape that is characterized by being about four times longer than wide and tapering to a point at the end.

LBM – Any of hundreds of "little brown mushrooms" that are commonly found and difficult to identify.

Legumes – Plants that bear seeds inside pods.

Lichen – A fungus and algae that are interconnected and live symbiotically.

Linear – A long, slender leaf shape.

Mode of action – Describes the chemistry and physiology of how a toxin or drug works in the body.

Monoecious – A plant that produces separate male and female flowers on the same plant.

Mutagenic – Any compound that causes damage to genetic information.

Mycelium – The collective mass of hyphal strands of a fungus (long, tubular filaments) that make up the vegetative body of a fungus.

Mycorrhizal – Describes a mutually beneficial relationship between a fungus and a plant.

Naturalized – The ecological status describing exotic species that have developed the capacity to reproduce and spread in locations where they have been introduced.

Neurotoxin – A category of toxins that damage the central nervous system.

Neurotransmitter – A chemical messenger that allows nerve cells to communicate.

Node – On a plant stem, the region where new leaves, stems, or buds will emerge.

Noxious – Any plant that causes harm to agricultural crops or natural habitats.

Opposite – A type of leaf arrangement where two leaves are attached per node and are arranged opposite each other along the stem.

Panicle – An inflorescence type characterized by flowers loosely arranged in a spike with many branches.

Parasite – An organism that persists by using another organism for nutrients and other aspects of survival.

Peltate – A leaf shape that is characterized as having a shield-like appearance.

Perennial – A plant that persists for multiple growing seasons.

Petiole – The stem-like attachment between a stem and the leaf.

Pinnate – A leaf that is subdivided into leaflets. Leaves can have multiple levels of such division.

Pistil – The female reproductive structures of the flowering plant, including a stigma, style, and ovary.

Pod – A fruit type characterized by being dry at maturity and dehiscent (splitting) along both sides to release seeds. Peas and beans produce pods.

Pome – A fruit type characterized by having a fleshy layer surrounding a core. An apple is a pome.

Protein – A category of chemical compounds characterized by having long chains of amino acids. In plants, proteins may include enzymes and other proteins that can have a biological effect on living cells, sometimes with poisonous or medicinal properties.

Raceme – An inflorescence characterized by having flowers arranged on a main stalk, attached on short stalks and equidistant from each other along the main stalk.

Ruminate – Typically, grazing animals that have four stomach compartments and a complex digestive process.

Sepal – The outer whorl of leaflike or petallike structures on a flower. Sepals typically surround the flower when it is in the bud.

Serrated – A leaf margin characterized by having a toothed or sawlike edge.

Sessile – Describing a leaf that is directly attached to the stem, with no petiole.

Silage – A crop that is harvested before drying and stored in an airtight system to allow for fermentation to occur. Typically used as animal feed.

Spadix – An inflorescence characterized by having small, inconspicuous flowers contained on a fleshy stem. Typically the spadix is surrounded by a larger, petallike structure called the spathe.

Spathe – A petallike structure that surrounds the spadix inflorescence in some plants.

Species – A hierarchical taxonomic rank of plants below genus.

Spike – An inflorescence characterized by having flowers arranged on a main stalk, directly attached to the stalk, and usually equidistant from each other.

Spp. – An abbreviated form of "species."

Stamen – The male reproductive structures of the flower, including the anthers that produce pollen.

Substrate – Used to describe the organic material fungi is found growing upon.

Symbiotic – A relationship between two or more organisms where the interaction between the organisms is mutually beneficial.

Taproot –A large, main root of a dicot plant.

Tepal – A floral structure that is either a petal or a sepal and that appears similar to both. Tepals are often observed in lily flowers, where the outermost whorl of the flower is made up of sepals that appear petallike.

Terpenoid – A class of chemical compounds derived from isoprene. Terpenes are often volatile in nature and aromatic. There is a significant interest in the potential of terpenes for their medicinal properties.

Trichome – A hairlike structure on the epidermis of a plant that can function as a protective structure in some plants.

Umbel – An inflorescence characterized by having flowers attached at a single point, which radiate out from this point like an umbrella.

Volva – A large membrane that covers many mushrooms in early growing stages. Remnants of the volva can provide helpful identification features.

Abrus precatorius

ROSARY PEA, JEQUIRITY BEAN

Abrus from the Ancient Greek word for delicate/graceful,
***precatorius* from the Latin word for praying.**

Fabaceae (Legume Family)

DESCRIPTION: *Abrus precatorius* is a perennial woody vine growing from a deep taproot, with slender, herbaceous branches. Leaves are alternate and pinnately compound, approximately 6–7 cm long, with 5–15 pairs of 3 cm–long leaflets. Flowers are small and pealike, growing in dense clusters from the leaf axils. The coloration is white to pink to pale violet. The seed pod is oblong and flat, reaching up to 5 cm long. Inside are 3–8 hard, shiny red seeds, superficially resembling a ladybug (without the spots).

DISTRIBUTION AND HABITAT: *Abrus precatorius* is native to India and parts of Asia, in tropical climates. It has been introduced as a garden ornamental in similar climates in North America, especially Florida, and is considered an invasive species in some parts of North America. In Florida, it has invaded pine forests and hammocks, crawling over native trees and shrubs.

TOXIC AGENT(S): All parts of the plant should be considered toxic, but seeds contain the highest concentrations of toxin. A toxalbumin called abrin is found in the seeds. It is a protein that disables ribosomes, thereby preventing protein synthesis in the cells. This causes cell death in multiple organ systems in the body. It has also been used as a poison, with a paste made from crushed seeds being applied to the sharp surfaces of weapons.

SIGNS AND SYMPTOMS OF POISONING: Exposure to toxins may occur through inhalation, mucous membranes, wounds, or ingestion. The seeds are sometimes used as jewelry, and it has been implicated in poisonings of those who make this jewelry, exposing themselves to the toxin when piercing the seeds to thread them. Children have been exposed to the toxin through jewelry products made from the seeds. Symptoms usually appear between several hours and several days after exposure, with the types of symptoms depending on the means of exposure. If inhaled, initial symptoms include fever, coughing, tightness in the chest, nausea, cyanosis (bluing of the skin), and pulmonary edema. Symptoms can then progress to excessive sweating and a drop in blood pressure, followed by shock and respiratory failure. If ingested, initial symptoms include nausea, vomiting, abdominal cramping, and difficulty swallowing. This progresses to signs of internal bleeding, such as bloody vomit and diarrhea, followed by a drop in blood pressure, drowsiness, stupor, and convulsions. Finally, multiorgan system failure sets in, accompanied by shock, vascular collapse, and death. Abrin can also be absorbed through the skin and through contact with the eyes, causing redness, pain, tearing, and bleeding from the eyes. If the exposure is large enough, it can then enter the bloodstream and affect all parts of the body.

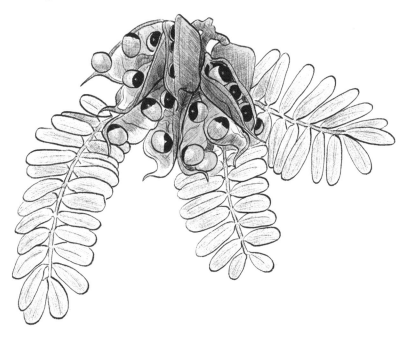

Aconitum spp.

WOLFSBANE, MONKSHOOD

Aconitum from the Greek word for dart (akon).

Ranunculaceae (Buttercup Family)

DESCRIPTION: *Aconitum* spp. are herbaceous perennials with a growth habit that can vary by species. Some species have an erect, upright form, and some species range from slightly spreading to almost vine-like. Leaves are arranged alternately on the stem and tend to be palmately divided into 3–7 segments. Flowers are either terminal or from leaf axils, arranged in panicles or racemes. The common name "Monkshood" references the unique flower shape, with the upper sepal forming a hoodlike structure that contains petals formed into a nectar spur inside. Flower color is blue in most species, though some are white or yellowish. Seeds are contained in dried fruits called follicles.

DISTRIBUTION AND HABITAT: The *Aconitum* genus includes a group of 100 species, five of which are native to North America. There are also many cultivated varieties that are popular garden flowers. Native species are found in temperate parts of North America outside of the Great Plains, and tend to occur in moist, shady wooded areas, such as ravines. Cultivated species can be expected throughout North America.

TOXIC AGENT(S): All parts of the plant are toxic, with roots reported to contain the highest concentrations of toxins. Plants contain the alkaloid aconitine. Aconitine interferes with the regulation of muscle contractions and neuron functions. Consuming 1 g of plant tissue is often enough to be a fatal dose. *Aconitum* is known as the "Queen of Poisons," and it is referenced in a myriad of historical, fictional, mythical, and magical accounts. For example, it has been suggested that the Viking warriors known as "berserkers" or "wolf heathens" used *Aconitum* to have a sensation of transforming into a bear or wolf and to reach a trancelike state of battle fury.

SIGNS AND SYMPTOMS OF POISONING: Exposure to toxins may occur externally through handling plant material, application of plant extracts to mucous membranes, or ingestion of dry or fresh plant material. Signs of intoxication can occur within 15 minutes and will vary based on the amount and method of ingestion. Signs may include confusion, crying, hallucination, gastrointestinal distress, muscle weakness, hypotension, heart palpitations, slowed, irregular, or accelerated heart rate, shortness of breath, sweating, headache, and death due to respiratory or cardiac failure.

Actaea spp.

BANEBERRY, DOLL'S EYES

Actaea from the Greek word for elderberry (aktea).

Ranunculaceae (Buttercup Family)

DESCRIPTION: *Actaea* spp. are herbaceous perennials that grow about 1.5 m tall. Leaves are divided, and leaflets are triangular and toothed. Small white flowers are clustered in spikes. Depending on the species, berries are white with dark spots (reminiscent of a doll's eye) or an attractive, shiny red.

DISTRIBUTION AND HABITAT: There are two *Actaea* species native to North America. Both species are broadly distributed throughout North America in shady, moist woodland habitats.

TOXIC AGENT(S): All *Actaea* species are toxic to varying degrees. Toxin concentrations will also vary due to growing conditions, season, and plant part. Roots and berries are believed to contain the highest levels of toxins. Like other plants within the Buttercup Family, *Actaea* spp. contain the glycoside ranunculin that is broken down into the toxin protoanemonin when plant tissue is wounded or macerated by chewing teeth. Protoanemonin has a bitter, acrid taste, which is likely the reason the *Actaea* berries are so bitter. It can bind to and inactivate several different proteins and can also transfer small molecules known as alkyl groups to DNA, causing DNA alkylation. Alkylated DNA causes mutations, disrupts cell division, and ultimately kills the cells. Protoanemonin is also known to disrupt the central nervous system. There is insufficient data in the published literature to ascertain what additional toxin(s) are present, but the toxicity of plant extracts on various insects and cell lines suggests a strong likelihood of additional toxins.

SIGNS AND SYMPTOMS OF POISONING: Most *Actaea* poisonings involve children attracted to the showy berries. Consumption will cause painful burning in the lining of the mouth and possibly the throat, nausea, and other gastrointestinal disturbances. Higher doses will cause a rapid heartbeat, throat constriction, intense abdominal and kidney pains, dizziness, and other disturbances, potentially including cardiac failure.

Adenium obesum

KUDU, DESERT ROSE

**Adenium refers to the Yemeni city of Aden,
obesum from the Latin word for plump (obesus).**

Apocynaceae (Dogbane Family)

DESCRIPTION: In its natural habit, *Adenium obesum* is a woody shrub with a notably large, bloated trunk, called a caudex. Stout branches are arranged in spirals around the stem. Leathery, oval leaves with prominent veins are clustered at the end of branches. It is probably most known for its large, tubular flowers. Flowers are typically pink with five petals. It is considered by many to be among the most beautiful plants for its unique and charming growth habit and prominent, showy flowers that can remain in bloom for most of the year.

DISTRIBUTION AND HABITAT: *Adenium obesum* is native to arid regions of eastern and southwestern Africa. It is frequently grown as an ornamental houseplant and bonsai in temperate climates and sparingly naturalized in arid regions of Mexico.

TOXIC AGENT(S): All parts of the plant and sap should be considered poisonous, although most published research on toxins has focused on the bark and sap. *Adenium obesum* also has an interesting history of use in the production of poison arrows and as a poison used in fishing. More recently, it has been used for aquaculture pond management, to kill undesirable fish before stocking desired species. The toxic agents include cardiac glycosides, triterpenoids, and steroids.

SIGNS AND SYMPTOMS OF POISONING: Poisoning may occur through handling wounded plants exuding sap or through ingestion. Symptoms will occur within 12–36 hours of exposure and will include possible irritation to the oral cavity, gastrointestinal disturbances, low heart rate and blood pressure, lethargy, coma, and possible death.

Aesculus spp.
Multiple based on species:

HORSE CHESTNUT, BUCKEYE, RED BUCKEYE

Aesculus is the Roman name for the Italian Oak (*Quercus frainetto*), and for reasons unknown, Carl Linnaeus used it to name this genus.

Sapindaceae (Soapberry Family)

DESCRIPTION: *Aesculus* is a deciduous shrub or tree reaching more than 30 m tall at maturity. Large, palmately compound leaves are one of its most characteristic features. Each leaf is composed of 5–7 leaflets. Leaflets have prominent veins and serrated leaf margins. It produces large clusters of showy, fragrant flowers in the spring and prominent, spiny fruits in the fall.

DISTRIBUTION AND HABITAT: There are six species of *Aesculus* native to North America. One of the most toxic species is Red Buckeye, *Aesculus pavia*, native to coastal North Carolina. *Aesculus* is found in woods, along streams, and often in disturbed habitats.

TOXIC AGENT(S): Seeds, bark, and new shoots are toxic and contain coumarin glycosides—specifically, aesculin, fraxin, and likely some undetermined toxins, possibly narcotic alkaloids. The precise mode of action of aesculin and fraxin is not entirely understood. They have neurotoxic properties at low concentration and are hemolytic (destroy red blood cells) at higher concentrations. Multiple reports also suggest the possibility of toxic alkaloid(s) in this species, but no specific alkaloids are described.

SIGNS AND SYMPTOMS OF POISONING: Exposure to toxins is almost always through ingestion of seeds, but there are a few reports of people grinding up dried seeds and using the powder as a form of snuff. Poisoning in humans most often occurs due to misidentification of Horse Chestnuts for the edible Chestnut, *Castanea* spp. Although death is not common, ingestion may result in oral ulcers, stumbling and trouble walking, muscle tremors, convulsions, and possibly death if medical intervention isn't received.

Agave lechuguilla

LECHUGUILLA

Agave **from the Ancient Greek word for noble/illustrious (agauos),**
lechuguilla **from the Spanish word for small lettuce.**

Asparagaceae (Asparagus Family)

DESCRIPTION: *Agave lechuguilla* is an evergreen with tough, fibrous, sword-shaped leaves (less than 1 m tall) that arise directly from the ground and have a very sharp and strong spine on the end that has been known to impale horses and puncture tires. After 12–15 years of growth, it produces a fast-growing, tall (5 m) flower stalk that bears dozens of yellow or purple flowers. After flowering and producing seeds, it dies.

DISTRIBUTION AND HABITAT: *Agave lechuguilla* is native to the Chihuahuan Desert and distributed in eastern Texas and northern Mexico. It is grown as a crop, providing the primary source of a tough, strong fiber known as Tampico. It is also found growing wild in the dry, rocky soils of the region.

TOXIC AGENT(S): All parts of the plant are toxic. The primary toxic agents in *Agave lechuguilla* are believed to be saponins and calcium oxalate crystals. The roots contain so much saponin, they were used by indigenous people of the Southwest to make soap. Toxicity in the saponins is reportedly activated by an unknown photodynamic agent. One saponin is believed to be hepatoxic (causing liver injury).

SIGNS AND SYMPTOMS OF POISONING: Exposure to toxins is through ingestion of dry or fresh plant material. Fatal poisoning is primarily observed in livestock, specifically sheep and goats, although cattle, horses, and other mammals including humans could be susceptible to poisoning. More fatalities are observed in high drought conditions, when consuming as little as 1% body weight is reported to cause lethal poisoning within one to two weeks. Initial indicators of poisoning may include listlessness, lethargy, loss of appetite, and ultimately coma and death due to liver failure.

Ageratina altissima

WHITE SNAKEROOT

**Ageratina from the Latin word for unaging,
altissima from the Latin word for tallest.**

Asteraceae (Aster Family)

DESCRIPTION: *Ageratina altissima* is a perennial plant, typically 50–80 cm tall, with a branching growth form. Stems are finely pubescent. Leaves are opposite and egg shaped, with serrated edges. Flowers are in flattened clusters at the tips of stems, white in color, and composed of numerous tiny flowers crowded together, giving the appearance of a single flower.

DISTRIBUTION AND HABITAT: *Ageratina altissima* is native to the eastern United States and widely distributed across the eastern two-thirds of North America. It is commonly found in woodlands, woodland edges, and disturbed areas.

TOXIC AGENT(S): This plant produces a mixture of toxins of various chemical types, but the alcohol tremetol is the most reported. Tremetol contains the poisonous ketone tremetone, which interferes with cellular respiration and causes myocardial degeneration and necrosis. It is responsible for a condition called milk sickness in humans and livestock. The toxins sicken the animals that eat fresh or dry plant material and accumulate in the milk and meat of animals that have consumed the plant material. The toxin is cumulative, meaning small amounts can be ingested over time, until a fatal dosage is reached. Milk sickness claimed many lives during the European settlement of North America, due to the settlers' lack of knowledge of the plant and its toxicity. Nancy Hanks Lincoln, the mother of Abraham Lincoln, may have died from milk sickness. An unnamed Shawnee woman and Dr. Anna Pierce Hobbs Bixby are credited with identifying and establishing *Ageratina altissima* as the cause of milk sickness in 1834, although neither was credited for this discovery until many decades later.

SIGNS AND SYMPTOMS OF POISONING: Exposure to toxins can occur through external contact with plant tissue, ingestion of plant material, or ingestion of meat or milk from cows that have consumed plant material. The most common symptoms in humans and animals are depression or inactivity, muscle tremors, weakness, nausea, vomiting, difficulty breathing, and acetone breath (ketosis). Death is reportedly agonizing, and decline may occur over several weeks.

Albizia julibrissin

SILK TREE, BASTARD TAMARIND, MIMOSA

Albizia for Filippo degli Albizzi,
julibrissin from the Persian word for silk flower.

Fabaceae (Legume Family)

DESCRIPTION: *Albizia julibrissin* is an attractive deciduous tree, growing up to 6 m tall with a crown spread up to double the height. The gray-green bark becomes striped with age. These trees produce leaves much later in the spring than other species. Leaves are feathery, bipinnately compound and can reach up to 45 cm in length. Individual leaflets are oblong in shape, and up to 1.5 cm in length. In the evening, the leaves fold up. The highly fragrant flowers are large , with white or pink silky threads creating a starburst appearance. The silky threads are the stamens, and the actual petals are small and nondescript. The fruit is a long (20 cm) pod with several seeds inside.

DISTRIBUTION AND HABITAT: *Albizia julibrissin* is originally native to parts of Asia, from Iran to Korea, but it has been widely planted as an ornamental tree around the world. It was brought to North America in the 18th century and is now distributed throughout southern North America. It can be found in disturbed areas, but preferentially grows in oak-hickory, pine, and riparian woodlands.

TOXIC AGENT(S): There are conflicting reports on the toxicity of the different parts of *Albizia julibrissin.* The seeds contain a neurotoxic alkaloid that counteracts vitamin B_6 in the body. Several other toxins or potential toxins have been isolated from bark and leaves, including the novel saponin julibroside, which is reported to alter brain receptors, but has promise as an antianxiety treatment at therapeutic doses.

SIGNS AND SYMPTOMS OF POISONING: Exposure to toxins is primarily through ingestion of green or mature seeds and pods. Signs of poisoning may be evident 12–24 hours after ingestion and include muscle twitching, myoclonic jerks, labored breathing, salivation, seizures, and death.

Ammi majus

BISHOP'S WEED, FALSE QUEEN ANNE'S LACE, BULLWORT, GREATER AMMI, LACE FLOWER

Ammi from the Greek word for sand (ammos), majus from the Latin word for big/grand/abundant.

Apiaceae (Carrot Family)

DESCRIPTION: *Ammi majus* is an herbaceous annual or biennial that grows to 2 m tall. It produces dainty, lacelike flowers on an umbel—in this type of inflorescence (flower arrangement), all flowers arise from a central point like an umbrella. Leaves are finely divided and feathery. The flowers and foliage are frequently used in the floral industry. The taproot will ultimately become large and carrot-like.

DISTRIBUTION AND HABITAT: *Ammi majus* is native to the Nile River Valley but is increasingly found in North America in naturalized populations, often along roadsides and ditches. It has been included in wildflower seed mixes distributed throughout North America. Due to morphological similarities to several other species in the Carrot Family, it is likely more widely distributed in North America than reports might suggest.

TOXIC AGENT(S): All parts of the plant are poisonous, but seeds contain the highest concentration of toxins. Like many plants, *Ammi majus* can be therapeutic in some applications and toxic in others, and it has been used medicinally by many cultures for thousands of years. There are reports of using the seeds for contraceptive purposes, and the fruits and leaves are used to treat skin disorders, particularly disorders relating to skin pigmentation. The plant contains furanocoumarins which bind with DNA in skin cells when exposed to UV light, causing severe tissue damage. Insoluble calcium oxalate crystals are contained in all parts of the plant and cause intense pain when consumed.

SIGNS AND SYMPTOMS OF POISONING: Exposure to toxins may occur through contact with plant sap or ingestion of plant material. External contact may cause severe dermatitis, and ingestion could be fatal. The most common signs of intoxication by *Ammi majus* are photosensitivity and phytophotodermatitis. Consumption will cause animals and humans to become highly photosensitive and shy away from light. The skin may appear sunburned and ultimately become swollen, develop large, oozing blisters, and slough off. Furanocoumarins found in *Ammi majus* can cause life-threatening effects by inhibiting gut enzymes that regulate pharmaceuticals in the bloodstream. This effect lasts for several days after consuming plant materials. It causes significant changes in the metabolic processing of over 30 common medications, including medicines that prevent blood clots and regulate blood pressure and heartbeat.

Argemone mexicana

MEXICAN POPPY, PRICKLY POPPY

Argemone from the Greek word for poppy-like plant, *mexicana* from the Spanish word for Mexican.

Papaveraceae (Poppy Family)

DESCRIPTION: *Argemone mexicana* is an annual species of poppy characterized by bright yellow poppy-like flowers that can reach 7 cm across. They are adorned on upright, branching plants that can reach 80 cm in height. Leaves are alternate and lobed, with clasping bases. Both the stems and leaves are usually armed with prickles. The fruits are capsules.

DISTRIBUTION AND HABITAT: *Argemone mexicana* is native to southern Florida and the Caribbean Islands, but it has been widely introduced throughout the world. In North America, it can be found along the coast from New England to Texas, and less commonly farther inland, across eastern North America. In North America, it tends to be found along roadsides, in fallow fields, and in other types of weedy waste places.

TOXIC AGENT(S): The primary toxins are the alkaloids sanguinarine and dihydrosanguinarine, which are found in the seeds. Other parts of the plant contain several other alkaloids, some with properties much like opium. Sanguinarine and dihydrosanguinarine cause cell death through the interference of enzymes involved in the transport of vital molecules across cell membranes.

SIGNS AND SYMPTOMS OF POISONING: Exposure to toxins can occur externally through skin and mucous membranes, or internally through ingestion of plant materials or extracts. External exposure to the caustic sap is not life-threatening but can cause necrosis of the skin and underlying tissues, leading to a thick scab called an eschar. Poisoning by ingestion tends to occur in areas where mustard seeds are cultivated, because Prickly Poppy can be a common weed in mustard fields and has similar-looking seeds. Ingestion of seeds or seed oil leads to a condition called epidemic dropsy. Clinical signs include swelling in extremities due to fluid buildup, headache, nausea, diarrhea, erythema, shortness of breath, and glaucoma. About 5% of cases end in mortality, usually due to heart or kidney failure, pneumonia, or respiratory distress.

Arnica spp.

ARNICA, LEOPARD'S BANE, MOUNTAIN SNUFF, CELTIC NARD, OTHERS

Unresolved It could be from the Arabic word for Leopard's Bane, the Latin word for lamb, or the Ancient Greek word for Sneezewort.

Asteraceae (Aster Family)

DESCRIPTION: *Arnica* is a perennial herb with yellow, daisy-like flowers that produce a head of bristly hairs when mature. Simple leaves are arranged opposite each other on most *Arnica* species, although some species also have or primarily have basal leaves. It is easy to identify a plant as an *Arnica*, being the only plant in North America with these characteristics. Still, more nuanced differences in morphological features can make identifying a specific *Arnica* species more challenging.

DISTRIBUTION AND HABITAT: At least 26 *Arnica* species are native to North America, with the greatest species diversity in western North America. *Arnica chamissonis*, found throughout most of western North America, is the species most like the European species, *A. montana*, that is commonly used in traditional medicine. Natural populations of these *Arnica* species are critically endangered in some areas due to over-harvesting to meet consumer demand for pharmaceuticals. Increasingly, suppliers are using "Mexican Arnica" (*Heterotheca inuloides*) to replace or supplement medicinal preparations reported to contain *Arnica*.

TOXIC AGENT(S): European and North American use of *Arnica* to treat contusions, inflammation, and general pain arose independently hundreds or even thousands of years ago. High-quality, peer-reviewed research on the efficacy of *Arnica* is mixed; some research suggests that the external application of *Arnica* on injuries may speed healing and reduce pain and inflammation. Other research indicates that external *Arnica* treatment increased pain compared to a placebo and did not improve healing speed or outcomes. Despite conflicting research on the efficacy, the external application of *Arnica* products is generally considered safe. *Arnica*-containing products should never be orally ingested, due to a toxic terpene called helenalin in the flowers and aerial parts of the plant. Specifically, helenalin is described as a toxic sesquiterpene lactone. Despite having known anti-inflammatory properties, and some intriguing antitumor properties, helenalin is toxic in part because it causes a reduction in an important antioxidant, glutathione. This significantly diminishes the ability of the liver to detoxify, resulting in liver damage or liver failure at even very low concentrations. Helenalin should be considered highly toxic. Roots and rhizomes do not contain helenalin, but they do contain thymol, a registered pesticide and antimicrobial. Thymol is generally regarded as safe for external exposure and inhalation, and is toxic but not fatal if swallowed.

SIGNS AND SYMPTOMS OF POISONING: Lethal exposure to toxins is primarily through ingestion of *Arnica*-containing products. Arnica ingestion may cause indigestion, vomiting, and other gastrointestinal disturbances at low doses. Toxic doses were more commonly reported following the consumption of tinctures containing *Arnica*; in these cases, ingestion has resulted in heart failure, liver failure, and other life-threatening outcomes.

Asclepias spp.

MILKWEED

Asclepias in honor of Asklepios, the Greek god of healing.

Apocynaceae (Dogbane Family)

DESCRIPTION: Milkweeds are easy to identify, as no other plant has flowers arranged and structured quite the same way. Flowers are arranged as an umbel—in this type of inflorescence (flower arrangement), all flowers arise from a central point like an umbrella. This arrangement creates a flat or curved top that allows a pollinator a landing spot and easy access to all flowers. The individual flowers are complex, composed of petals positioned backward to reveal a unique structure called the corona. The star-shaped corona is made up of five individual units that each contain a waxy cluster of pollen called a pollinium. Pollinia attach to the body or legs of a pollinator and are thus efficiently carried to new plants.

DISTRIBUTION AND HABITAT: The *Asclepias* genus contains 35 North American species and over 200 species worldwide. Milkweeds are named for the toxic milky latex that exudes from wounds on all plant parts. *Asclepias* species are distributed across nearly all of North America in various habitats. The most toxic species are those with narrow leaves that are whorled around the stem (narrow verticillate leaves). Of these, the "Utah Milkweed" (*Asclepias labriformis*) is reported to be among the most toxic plants of the Western Range. *A. labriformis* is found in Utah, where it can be observed in the sandy plains and plateaus that often serve as rangeland.

TOXIC AGENT(S): Although all *Asclepias* species contain poisonous sap, there is great variability in toxicity among species, in different parts of the plant, and at varying times of the year. Early shoots and pods are reported to contain the least toxins. Most milkweeds produce cardiac glycosides (cardenolides). These function by interfering with cell membrane potential. They have historically been used at therapeutic doses to increase the strength of heartbeat contractions while reducing heart rate to create a more efficient cardiac output. Due to the severity of side effects, including death, cardiac glycosides are no longer regularly used to treat congestive heart failure and arrhythmias. Some milkweeds also contain a probable neurotoxic agent found in the milky latex called galitoxin, a resinoid. The mode of action of galitoxin is not understood, and the effects are cumulative.

SIGNS AND SYMPTOMS OF POISONING: Lethal exposure to toxins is almost exclusively due to consuming milkweed plants. Fatal milkweed poisoning in humans is possible but very rare. There are a few recent cases of people eating improperly prepared fried milkweed pods, but in each of these cases the victim received timely medical care and did not have serious long-term consequences. However, there are numerous and frequent cases of animal death due to milkweed consumption, primarily among grazing animals and domestic pets. Signs in animals may include weakness, tremors and nervousness, collapse, labored breathing, coma, and death.

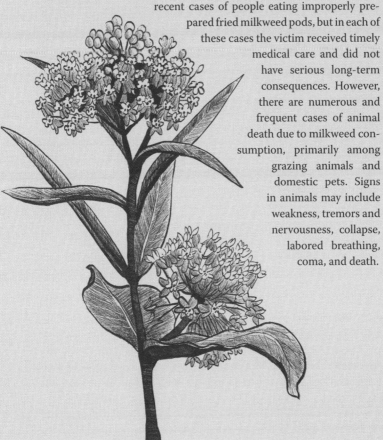

Astragalus spp.

LOCOWEED, MILK VETCH

Astragalus from the Greek word for anklebone (astragalos).

Fabaceae (Legume Family)

DESCRIPTION: *Astragalus* is an annual or perennial herbaceous legume. Most species have pinnately divided leaves with a light to wooly covering of hairs over the leaf and stem surfaces. The purple or yellow flowers are clustered on racemes and have the shape of a typical pea flower, with a banner, wings, and keel. Seeds are usually contained in a pod.

DISTRIBUTION AND HABITAT: *Astragalus* is a large genus, including over 2,000 species worldwide. At least 375 of these species are found in North America. *Astragalus* is widely distributed across North America in a broad array of habitats. A great diversity of *Astragalus* species can be found in the mountainous and desert regions of the western United States.

TOXIC AGENT(S): There are three primary toxicity factors in *Astragalus*, including: swainsonine, nitro-containing toxins, and promotion of selenium accumulation. Not all *Astragalus* species have all toxicity factors. Swainsonine is most likely not produced by *Astragalus*, but instead produced by a fungus that lives inside the plant. Swainsonine functions in part by preventing the breakdown of certain small sugar molecules; these molecules build up inside the cell, disrupting normal cell function and potentially killing the cell. The primary nitro-containing toxin is miserotoxin, which is only toxic in animals with a ruminant digestion—animals that do not completely chew the vegetation they eat, storing it instead as balls of "cud" to be eaten later. Bacteria in the guts of ruminants may cause the breakdown of miserotoxin and release of a toxic nitrogen compound known as nitropropanol. Selenium toxicity is only a problem in those *Astragalus* species growing in areas with high levels of selenium. This would include areas of western Canada and the western United States.

SIGNS AND SYMPTOMS OF POISONING: Swainsonine is a cumulative poison—although this could theoretically affect any mammals, it primarily affects livestock animals who have consumed toxic plants over a period of weeks or months. Once an animal shows signs of "locoweed poisoning," it is usually too late. Signs may include odd behavior (hence "loco"), loss of coordination, miscarriage, and ultimately death. Miserotoxin poisoning only affects ruminant animals. Signs include progressive muscle weakness, severe respiratory distress, coma, and sometimes death. Selenium toxicity may be chronic or acute, depending on the dose and method of exposure. In chronic poisoning, early signs may include weak nails, brittle hair, and bad breath. Acute poisoning usually involves higher doses than would be consumed from selenium-containing plant material, and signs may include shortness of breath, pulmonary edema, uncoordinated movements, paralysis, loss of appetite, and possibly death.

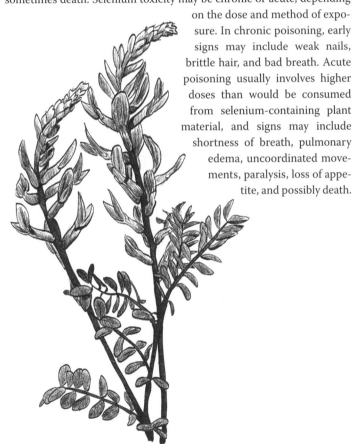

Astrolepis cochisensis

JIMMY FERN, SCALY CLOAK FERN

Astrolepis from the Greek words for star (astron) and scale (lepis), cochisensis refers to Cochise County, Arizona.

Pteridaceae (Brake Family)

DESCRIPTION: *Astrolepis cochisensis* is a true fern with leaves up to 40 cm long. Leaves are composed of up to 50 pairs of oblong pinnae (leaflets) that are 4–7 mm long. The lower surface of the pinnae is nearly completely covered by fuzzy-looking, 1 mm–wide ovate (egg-shaped) scales. Similar but more circular-shaped scales are on the upper surface, but they are very sparse and tend to fall off. Ferns do not produce a flower, fruit, or seed.

DISTRIBUTION AND HABITAT: *Astrolepis cochisensis* is found in Arizona, California, New Mexico, Oklahoma, Texas, and Mexico. It is found primarily in desert and scrub habitats.

TOXIC AGENT(S): The toxic agents in *Astrolepis cochisensis* are yet to be discovered. There are not many reported toxins in ferns and no toxins reported in ferns that are closely related to Jimmy Fern. Determining the toxins in *Astrolepis cochisensis* will be an interesting discovery for a future plant scientist.

SIGNS AND SYMPTOMS OF POISONING: Exposure to poison occurs after any appreciable amount of plant material is ingested. Poisoning most often occurs after a rainy period. Animals that have consumed the fern typically show signs of intoxication within 10–60 minutes. Signs do not begin until animals walk or run after eating plant material. Signs may include incoordination, rapid pulse, gasping, prostration, and trembling, called "The Jimmies." When death occurs, it is due to respiratory paralysis. Animals take a few additional steps, gasp, and collapse. Effects on humans are not yet known.

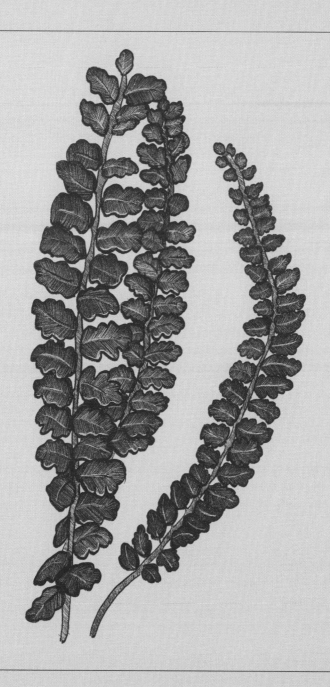

Atropa belladonna

DEADLY NIGHTSHADE

**Atropa from the Greek word for inflexible/unchangeable (atropos),
and the name for one of the three Fates, responsible for
determining the manner of a person's death,
belladonna from the Italian word for beautiful lady.**

Solanaceae (Nightshade Family)

DESCRIPTION: *Atropa belladonna* is a perennial with a shrubby growth habit. Plants reach about 2 m tall at maturity. Leaves are in pairs arranged alternately along the stem. One leaf of each pair is large (20 cm), and one is smaller (6 cm). Flowers are purple and bell-shaped, approximately 3 cm long. Berries are an appealing, shiny black at maturity.

DISTRIBUTION AND HABITAT: *Atropa belladonna* is originally native to southern Europe and parts of Asia but has naturalized throughout many parts of the world. In North America, there are reports of naturalized populations in New York, Michigan, California, Oregon, and Washington. It is also widely grown in cultivation. In its native range, *A. belladonna* is found in the understory of woodlands, preferring the chalky soils of southern Europe. In naturalized populations, it is found in many different habitats; in North America, it can be found in dumps, quarries, and other disturbed areas.

TOXIC AGENT(S): *Atropa belladonna* is one of the most well-known killer plants. It has been used for millennia for a wide range of human applications—including the often-reported external application to eyes to make them appear larger and more appealing, for a variety of medicinal purposes, and more nefarious (even homicidal) applications. All plant parts should be considered poisonous, but more reported poisonings have occurred after consuming berries. The toxic anticholinergic alkaloids found in *A. belladonna* include atropine, hyoscyamine, and scopolamine. These alkaloids can block chemical messages sent by the neurotransmitter acetylcholine. These messages are required for the normal function of the body and brain.

SIGNS AND SYMPTOMS OF POISONING: Lethal exposure to toxins is primarily through ingestion, but external application to mucous membranes can also be fatal. Symptoms of poisoning occur very quickly after consumption—they may include delirium and hallucinations. In children, this may manifest as saying nonsensical things and general confusion and disorientation. Poisoning will cause dilated pupils, a rapid heartbeat, and possibly death due to respiratory failure.

Bassia scoparia

FALSE CYPRESS, SUMMER CYPRESS, KOCHIA, MEXICAN FIREWEED, BURNING BUSH

***Bassia* honors Italian botanist Ferdinando Bassi (1710–1774), *scoparia* is from the Latin word for sweeper (scoparius).**

Amaranthaceae (Amaranth Family)

DESCRIPTION: *Bassia scoparia* is an annual forb (a plant other than a grass) that grows up to 3 m tall, with a bushy growth form that is round or pyramidal in shape, due to the habit of its side branches ascending and curving upward. The bright green leaves are alternate in arrangement, and typically lance-linear in shape, up to 10 cm long and 2 cm wide, turning red in the fall. Stems can be green to reddish and finely ribbed. Parts of the plant often break off and form tumbleweeds. The flowers are inconspicuous and found along the stems in the leaf axils.

DISTRIBUTION AND HABITAT: *Bassia scoparia* is a Eurasian native that has become established across a large portion of North America, especially in the Western and Great Plains regions, primarily in open or disturbed habitats. It has the capacity to quickly become an invasive species in some areas, due to its ability to grow in very harsh and dry conditions, and quickly spread via tumbleweeds.

TOXIC AGENT(S): *Bassia scoparia* can accumulate high levels of nitrate and oxalate, which can be toxic if consumed in large quantities. Saponins and alkaloids are also present, though their effects are not well established. Nitrate gets converted to nitrite during digestion. Once it is in the bloodstream, nitrite combines with hemoglobin, forming methemoglobin, which is unable to transport oxygen, resulting in suffocation and death if a lethal dose is consumed. Oxalates combine with calcium in the body to form the insoluble calcium oxalate, which can then accumulate in the kidneys, leading to kidney failure.

SIGNS AND SYMPTOMS OF POISONING: Exposure to toxins is exclusively through consumption of fresh or dry plant material, often over the course of multiple weeks. This plant is primarily of concern to livestock, as humans normally do not consume much, if any, of this plant. In cases of nitrate poisoning, symptoms include bluish or brownish mucous membranes, abnormal breathing, elevated pulse rate, salivation, weakness, tremors, and coma. Abortions can occur 10–14 days after consumption. Oxalate poisoning leads to symptoms such as lower back pain, blood in the urine, excessive thirst, edema, fatigue, nausea, vomiting, and loss of appetite.

Brugmansia spp.

ANGEL'S TRUMPET

**Brugmansia in honor of Dutch botanist
Sebald Justinus Brugmans (1763–1819).**

Solanaceae (Nightshade Family)

DESCRIPTION: The *Brugmansia* genus includes seven species, all of which are toxic. The collective common name for this genus, "Angel's Trumpet," refers to the large, pendulous flowers that can be up to 50 cm long and 35 cm wide. The showy flowers vary from red, white, yellow, green, or orange, and they have an alluring fragrance that tends to be most noticeable after sunset. They grow as shrubs or small trees with semiwoody stems, ranging in height from 3 m to 11 m. Large, often slightly hairy leaves alternate on each side of the stem.

DISTRIBUTION AND HABITAT: This genus originated in the tropics of South America but is listed as "Extinct in the Wild" by the International Union for Conservation of Nature (IUCN). No populations of *Brugmansia* exist from an original wild source. It is found in naturalized populations throughout the world, including tropical regions of North America, as the result of escaped cultivated plants. Due to its beauty, rapid growth, and easy cultivation, *Brugmansia* is a popular ornamental throughout North America. It can survive in hardiness zones 9 and above.

TOXIC AGENT(S): All *Brugmansia* species should be considered highly toxic, and the ingestion of even one seed would be a cause for concern. All parts of the plant are poisonous. Roots, seeds, and leaves are reported to contain the highest concentrations of toxic compounds, but even the pollen of this genus is toxic. The most frequently reported source of poisoning is the consumption of flowers. At least 59 different alkaloids have been isolated from *Brugmansia* species, with atropine and scopolamine believed to be responsible for the most severe consequences of ingestion. These alkaloids inhibit nerve impulses for involuntary muscle movement and other bodily functions.

SIGNS AND SYMPTOMS OF POISONING: Exposure to toxins may occur through handling plant material, especially sap, smoke inhalation of dried plant material, eating raw plant material, or drinking teas made from dried plant material. Postingestion symptoms will occur rapidly and may include pupil dilation, inability to focus vision, decreased sweating, increased heart rate, auditory and visual hallucinations, possible acute psychosis, coma, and death.

Calla palustris

CALLA, WILD CALLA, WATER ARUM

**Calla from the Greek word for beauty (kallos),
palustris from the Latin word for bog (paluster).**

Araceae (Arum Family)

DESCRIPTION: *Calla palustris* is an aquatic, perennial herb. It is easily recognized by its unique floral structure composed of two primary parts called a spathe and a spadix. The spathe is a modified leaf that creates a protective sheath around the flowers. The flowers are contained along a stem-like stalk called the spadix. In *Calla palustris*, the spathe is broad and white. The flowers covering the spadix are green until yellow anthers emerge. Leaves are heart shaped, and the plant grows in a sprawling habit.

DISTRIBUTION AND HABITAT: *Calla palustris* is native to North America. It is distributed throughout most of Canada and the north-central and northeastern United States. It is primarily found in aquatic environments, preferring shallow wetlands, including marshes and bogs.

TOXIC AGENT(S): *Calla palustris* leaves contain very high levels of insoluble calcium oxalate in the form of needlelike structures called raphides. Many plants contain oxalates, and they are one of the most frequent sources of nonlethal plant poisonings. Insoluble oxalates are crystallized calcium and oxalic acid; in the plant, they may serve as a defense against herbivory. Plants may also have soluble oxalates that do not become crystallized until after ingestion, causing a different and usually more severe systemic response.

SIGNS AND SYMPTOMS OF POISONING: Exposure to toxins is primarily via ingestion of plants. The sharp calcium crystals of insoluble oxalates cause intense pain and gastrointestinal distress. In very rare cases, swelling of the laryngeal area and epiglottis may occur, resulting in possible death by suffocation. There is only one reported case of this happening in a dog who consumed *Calla palustris*, who fortunately received a tracheotomy and survived. Soluble oxalates may cause chronic or acute poisoning. In chronic poisoning, soluble oxalates bind to available calcium and cause nutrient deficiencies over time. In acute poisoning, soluble oxalates form calcium crystals that accumulate in the kidneys and cause kidney failure and death.

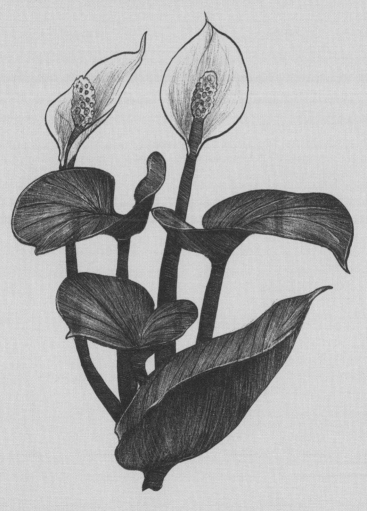

Cercocarpus montanus

MOUNTAIN MAHOGANY

Cercocarpus from the Greek words for tail (kerkos) and fruit (carpus), *montanus* from the Latin word for mountain.

Rosaceae (Rose Family)

DESCRIPTION: *Cercocarpus montanus* is not a true Mahogany, but a scrubby, broadleaf evergreen shrub or small tree, reaching about 4 m tall and 2 m wide. Leaves are simple, with prominent veins and serrated margins. Flowers are small and inconspicuous. Seeds produce a long and characteristic feathery awn, making this species easy to identify.

DISTRIBUTION AND HABITAT: *Cercocarpus montanus* is distributed throughout much of the western United States. Its preferred habitat includes the low hills of the Rocky Mountains, the Great Plains, and the chaparral scrub biome of the western United States.

TOXIC AGENT(S): *Cercocarpus montanus* contains cyanogenic glycosides that release cyanide during the digestion process. All parts of the plant are toxic, and the toxin is always present in the plant. Dangerous concentrations are found in dried or cut leaves. Cyanide prevents the release of oxygen from hemoglobin, leading to anoxia. Toxic levels of some heavy metals have also been reported, which may be a contributing toxicity factor.

SIGNS AND SYMPTOMS OF POISONING: Exposure to toxins is through ingestion of dry or fresh plant materials, but most fatal poisonings in livestock occur while grazing on dried plant material. Ruminant animals appear to be most susceptible to poisoning, likely due to bacteria in the ruminate digestion. Cyanide is fast acting, and signs of poisoning will within withing minutes of reaching the lethal dose. These include tremors, weakness, dizziness, vertigo, and difficulty breathing, progressing to coma and death within 15 minutes to several hours.

Cicuta aculate

WATER HEMLOCK, SPOTTED COWBANE, SUICIDE ROOT

**Cicuta from the Latin word for Hemlock,
aculate from the Latin word for spotted.**

Apiaceae (Carrot Family)

DESCRIPTION: *Cicuta aculate* is an herbaceous perennial plant with hollow stems, reaching up to 1.5 m in height. Stems are hairless and often have purple spots or streaks. Leaves are pinnately compound, with shiny green, lanceolate leaflets with serrated edges. Leaf veins are forked at the tip, with one vein terminating at the notch between the teeth, and the other at the tip of the leaflet. This can help distinguish it from Poison Hemlock, *Conium maculatum*, which has leaf veins that extend to the tip of the tooth. White flowers are borne in compound umbels, like other members of the Carrot Family. The thick, white roots smell like parsnip and have internal chambers.

DISTRIBUTION AND HABITAT: *Cicuta aculate* is native to all of North America and is distributed from northern Mexico northward. It is primarily a wetland plant, found in wet prairies, along lakeshores, in swamps, etc.

TOXIC AGENT(S): *Cicuta aculate* is considered one of the most toxic plants in North America. All parts of the plant contain cicutoxin and oenanthotoxin, but roots in the spring contain the highest concentration. Although well-known, the precise mode of action of these toxins is not understood. They are believed to interfere with the function of GABA, a neurotransmitter that blocks the impulses between the nerve cell and the brain. Inhibition of GABA can result in a cascade of consequences, including seizures and death.

SIGNS AND SYMPTOMS OF POISONING: THERE IS NO SAFE LEVEL OF CONSUMPTION. Exposure to toxins is through ingestion of plant materials; in many cases, this is due to misidentification of the plant as a safe forage plant. A 2–3 cm segment of root material is reported to cause fatalities in adult humans. There are reports of children being fatally poisoned from just putting plant stems into their mouths when using the hollow stems as whistles or peashooters. Multiple deaths occur annually due to accidental ingestion of *Cicuta aculate.* The first symptoms can appear as soon as 15 minutes after consumption, and include convulsions and seizures, vomiting, salivation, and sweating. The heart rate may slow or speed up, followed by respiratory failure, which is usually the cause of death.

Colchicum autumnale

AUTUMN CROCUS, MEADOW SAFFRON, NAKED LADY

Colchicum from the Ancient Greek name for the region of modern-day Georgia, *autumnale* means "autumn flowering" and originates from the Latin word autumnus.

(Colchicum Family)

DESCRIPTION: There are two plants with the common name Autumn Crocus. Both plants bloom at the same time and have similar flowers. However, there is an essential distinction between the two species: edible saffron is made from the anthers of one species (*Crocus sativus*), while all parts of the other (*Colchicum autumnale*) contain a deadly toxin. This is an excellent example of why we learn and use the scientific names of plants. Although frequently referred to as a "crocus," *Colchicum autumnale* is NOT a true crocus. Like *Crocus sativus*, it does arise from a corm and has a similar simple, six-petaled flower that may be pink, purple, or white. Unlike *Crocus sativus*, *Colchicum autumnale* produces dark green leaves that look similar to the leaves of the tulip but are only present in the spring. The *Colchicum* leaves die back by summer, and flowers on leafless stalks emerge in the fall. For this reason, they are sometimes referred to as "Naked Ladies." *Colchicum autumnale* is further distinguished by having larger flowers with six stamens, while *Crocus sativus* produces a daintier flower with only three stamens.

DISTRIBUTION AND HABITAT: *Colchicum autumnale* is native to Great Britain and Ireland, with naturalized populations in the northeastern United States and smaller naturalized populations in the northwestern United States. It is one of the most common commercially available fall garden bulbs and is extensively cultivated across North America. It is hardy in zones 5–9.

TOXIC AGENT(S): *Colchicum autumnale* contains the highly toxic alkaloid colchicine. All plant parts should be considered toxic, but the highest colchicine concentrations are typically found in the seeds. Colchicine is an interesting alkaloid, and the complete mode of action is not entirely understood. On a molecular level, it arrests cell division, and cells exposed to colchicine often have unusual nuclear configurations. In fact, plant breeders have used colchicine in some breeding programs to create plants with doubled chromosome numbers, which can be a desirable trait for a variety of reasons.

SIGNS AND SYMPTOMS OF POISONING: Exposure to toxins may occur through handling plant material, inhaling volatilized toxins, or ingestion. Accidental ingestion is by far the most common route for fatal poisonings. Consumption of any amount of *Colchicum autumnale* is extremely dangerous. There are three phases in colchicine poisoning. The first phase occurs within 24 hours of ingestion and is characterized by abdominal pain and increasing gastrointestinal distress. The second phase may last up to five to seven days and is characterized by muscle weakness and internal organ failure. If the patient survives phase two, they may experience phase three, which is characterized by hair loss, fever, bruising, exhaustion, and extreme weakness. There are multiple reports of foragers mistaking *Colchicum autumnale* for wild garlic. In all reported cases, hospitalization was required, and some cases were ultimately fatal.

Colubrina texensis

TEXAS SNAKEWOOD, TEXAS HOG PLUM

Colubrina from the Latin word for snake (colubra), *texensis* for Texas.

Rhamnaceae (Buckthorn Family)

DESCRIPTION: This is a round shrub that can reach 25 cm in height and width and tends to form dense thickets. It has zigzagging stems that are a light gray in color, while mature bark resembles snakeskin. In spring, small, greenish star-shaped flowers appear, followed by dark red to black fruits. Leaves are small and elliptical in shape, colored grayish green. Young leaves are hairy, but the hairs fall off by the time the leaf matures.

DISTRIBUTION AND HABITAT: *Colubrina texensis* is only found in the central and south central parts of Texas and adjacent parts of Mexico. It grows in dry, gravelly, or rocky slopes and along arroyos.

TOXIC AGENT(S): The toxic agents in *Colubrina* are not known. It is possible it produces toxins like those found in other members of the Buckthorn Family. These include four different anthracenone toxins, also referred to as "Buckthorn Toxins." In toxic species, all parts of the plant contain anthracenone toxins, but the highest concentrations are found in the mature fruit. These toxins are believed to cause the loss of the protective fatty layer that surrounds nerve cells. Demyelinated nerve cells have a diminished ability to send electrical impulses, causing muscle weakness and paralysis.

SIGNS AND SYMPTOMS OF POISONING: Exposure to toxins is primarily due to accidental ingestion of berries, most frequently reported in children. Poisoning from consumption can be very difficult to diagnose because symptoms mimic several other chronic conditions. Signs of poisoning may manifest one to ten days after consuming berries. *Colubrina* is also poisonous to animals. Livestock losses due to consumption of berries and leaves is known to occur, especially in sheep.

Conium maculatum

POISON HEMLOCK

Conium from the Ancient Greek word kóneion, which might
mean cone, liquid pitch, or "to spin or whirl,"
maculatum from the Latin word for spot.

Apiaceae (Carrot Family)

DESCRIPTION: *Conium maculatum* is a biennial herb that reaches
about 3 m tall. The thick stem is hollow, hairless, and covered with purple
streaks; these features are useful in helping to distinguish this genus from
other similar genera in the Carrot Family, but should not be used as a
definitive identifying characteristic. Leaves are three or four times pinnate and lacy with a triangular form. Flowers are small, white, and clustered into large umbels at the top of the plant. Extreme caution should be
used with this plant. *Conium maculatum* is frequently misidentified as
one of various nontoxic, edible plants in the Carrot Family, resulting in
sometimes fatal consequences.

DISTRIBUTION AND HABITAT: *Conium maculatum* is native to
Europe, North Africa, and tropical regions of Asia. It is now distributed
globally and is a noxious weed found throughout North America. It is
often found in disturbed areas, particularly on wet, poorly drained soils.
It is frequently observed along streams, roadsides, and edges of agricultural fields.

TOXIC AGENT(S): All plant parts should be considered toxic, with
the highest concentration of toxic alkaloids believed to be in the early
spring. There are multiple toxic alkaloids in *Conium maculatum*, all
derived from the same alkaloid precursor, γ-coniceine. These alkaloids
function like nicotine; at low doses, they stimulate cholinergic acetylcholine receptors, and at toxic doses, the receptors become overstimulated
and shut down. When these receptors are blocked, it results in serious
impairment of the nervous and neuromuscular systems.

SIGNS AND SYMPTOMS OF POISONING: Poisoning may occur through inhalation or ingestion. Accidental ingestion due to mistaken plant identification is almost always the cause of serious poisonings in people. The first symptoms of intoxication may occur as early as 30 minutes after consumption, and include drowsiness, a burning feeling in the digestive tract, and a slow heartbeat after initial exposure, followed by a rapid heartbeat, muscle twitches, trembling, coma, and death.

Convallaria majalis

LILY OF THE VALLEY

Convallaria **from the Latin word for valley,**
majalis **from the Latin word for May.**

Liliaceae (Lily Family)

DESCRIPTION: *Convallaria majalis* is a low-growing perennial. Plants tend to grow in large clusters, due to extensive spreading via underground stems (rhizomes). Individual plants have two leaves and an arching stem of small, white, bell-shaped flowers. Flowers are highly fragrant and used in the perfume industry.

DISTRIBUTION AND HABITAT: The majority of Lily of the Valley plants growing in North America are naturalized escapes from Eurasia. There is a very similar, but rare, North American native species, equally toxic, found growing in the Appalachians: *Convallaria pseudomajalis*. Both species prefer growing in shady woodlands.

TOXIC AGENT(S): All parts of the plant should be considered toxic. There are over 30 cardiac glycosides isolated from *Convallaria majalis*; the most toxic is reported to be convallatoxin. It functions in a manner almost indistinguishable from the well-known cardiac glycoside, digitalis—with the interesting exception that convallatoxin is less cumulative and has a possibly broader therapeutic range. Like other cardiac glycosides, convallatoxin works by interfering with cell membrane potential. It has historically been used at therapeutic doses to increase the strength of heartbeat contractions while reducing heart rate to create a more efficient cardiac output.

SIGNS AND SYMPTOMS OF POISONING: Small children and pets are at greatest risk of poisoning. Case studies indicate it is difficult to ascertain how much and which parts of the plant will result in serious or lethal poisonings. One case reported that a young child consumed at least 15 ripened berries and experienced only vomiting. In a different case, a young child chewed on a single leaf and had multiple instances of atrioventricular (AV) block—a situation where the heart beats irregularly and much more slowly—stopping for up to 20 seconds. Signs of overdose may include sweating, light-headedness, slow heartbeat, low blood pressure, and general gastrointestinal disturbances. Death may be caused by respiratory failure or arrhythmias.

Corydalis spp.

YELLOW CORYDALIS

Corydalis from the Latin word for crested lark (corydalus).

Papaveraceae (Poppy Family)

DESCRIPTION: *Corydalis* spp. can be annual or perennial, and tend to be weak-stemmed plants growing from rhizomes or tubers. Leaves can be simple, but are usually compound, with 2–6 leaflets. Flowers are diverse in color and shape, but tend to be tubular and bilaterally symmetrical.

DISTRIBUTION AND HABITAT: *Corydalis* is a group of about 100 species found throughout temperate areas of North America, Eurasia, and Africa, ten of which may be found in North America. Many of the species are cultivated as ornamentals and have established themselves outside of their native ranges. They can be found throughout most of North America, other than arid regions of the Great Plains and deserts of southern North America. The different species can be found in a variety of habitats, with moist woods and dry, rocky, wooded areas being among the most common.

TOXIC AGENT(S): All parts of the plant are toxic and contain the alkaloids bulbocapnine, and corydaline, as well as several others. These alkaloids have a broad range of effects on the body, leading to several species of *Corydalis* being used in traditional medicines, usually as a sedative or analgesic. However, in high enough doses, these compounds have the potential to be toxic to humans, pets, and other animals.

SIGNS AND SYMPTOMS OF POISONING: Exposure to toxins is primarily though ingestion of fresh or dry plant material. Clinical signs of *Corydalis* poisoning include nausea, dizziness, fatigue, rapid breathing, and convulsions. In lethal doses, the heart rate and breathing slow down, accompanied by convulsions.

Crotalaria spp.

RATTLEBOX

Crotalaria **from the Greek word for rattle or castanet (krotalon).**

Fabaceae (Legume Family)

DESCRIPTION: There are many species in the *Crotalaria* genus. All species are nitrogen-fixing, herbaceous annuals or perennials with yellow, pealike flowers on long, terminal clusters. The seeds are contained in inflated pods that rattle when dried; hence the name Rattlebox.

DISTRIBUTION AND HABITAT: *Crotalaria* is a large genus of more than 700 species; some species are used as a food source for humans and animals, some are grown as ornamentals, and some are grown for their use as a nitrogen-fixing cover crop. The greatest species diversity is in Africa, where over 400 *Crotalaria* species have been identified. About a dozen *Crotalaria* species can be found in North America. Seven of these species are native, and a handful were intentionally brought to North America from Africa and India in the early 20th century as nitrogen-fixing cover crops. Unfortunately, several of these exotic *Crotalaria* species are now listed as noxious invasive weeds in parts of North America, causing significant livestock and crop loss. *Crotalaria* species are most abundant from Mexico to the southeast United States and the Atlantic coast. They can also be found in parts of the western and midwestern United States.

TOXIC AGENT(S): All parts of the plant are toxic. The pyrrolizidine alkaloids monocrotaline and spectabiline are responsible for the toxicity of *Crotalaria*. Some species produce both alkaloids, and some produce only one, with species producing only monocrotaline reported to be the most toxic. When these alkaloids are metabolized in the liver, they are converted to highly reactive pyrroles that cause cellular dysfunction, disrupt cell division, and kill cells. This damage can be cumulative, ultimately obstructing the venous system, leading to liver failure, and potentially multiorgan failure. They may also cause pulmonary hypertension.

SIGNS AND SYMPTOMS OF POISONING:

Exposure to toxins is primarily through repeated ingestion of dry or fresh plant materials over a period of several weeks. Edible cereal grains mixed with seeds from weedy *Crotalaria* species is reported as the cause of significant human mortalities in at least one case in Sarjuga, India, resulting in 67 human deaths. Human disease and mortality caused by *Crotalaria* species are likely under-reported. Livestock losses can also be significant. Signs of poisoning typically occur over the course of several weeks. Signs include abdominal swelling and pain, enlarged liver, loss of appetite, nausea, vomiting, and diarrhea.

Cycas spp.

SAGO PALM

Cycas from the Greek word kukas, which is a mistranscription of the word koikas, which refers to a type of palm tree.

Cycadaceae (Cycad Family)

DESCRIPTION: Sago Palm is a name given to three species of Cycad that are a source of the starchy food called sago. They are small trees, up to 10 m in height, that outwardly resemble palm trees. The leaves resemble palm fronds and are glossy green in color, growing in a rosette from the top of the stem. Individual leaves can reach several feet in length on mature trees. Individual trees are either male or female, with both producing large (up to 1 m) cone-like reproductive structures at the top of the stem. Male cones are usually larger than female cones.

DISTRIBUTION AND HABITAT: *Cycas* spp. are found naturally in tropical regions from Southeast Asia and Australia to eastern Africa, but are widely grown as ornamentals worldwide. There are naturalized populations of *Cycas* in hardiness zones 10 and 11.

TOXIC AGENT(S): All parts of the Sago Palm contain the glycosides cycasin and macrozamin and the neurotoxic amino acid β-methylamino l-alanine (BMAA). The toxins can be found in most parts of the plant, but are most concentrated in the seeds. Cycasin and macrozamin are acted upon by enzymes found in the stomachs of mammals that cause the formation of methylazoxymethanol (MAM), which then breaks down into formaldehyde and diazomethane. This irritates the GI tract and causes liver cell necrosis. In addition, diazomethane also methylates DNA, which is potentially carcinogenic. BMAA is produced by symbiotic blue-green algae that live in Cycad roots. The BMAA mode of action is not fully understood, but involves the dysfunction and death of motor neurons. It is thought to be the cause of lytico-bodig disease, which is endemic to the Chamorro people on the island of Guam, who eat bats that feed on Cycad seeds. The condition has similarities to ALS, Parkinson's, and Alzheimer's.

SIGNS AND SYMPTOMS OF POISONING: Exposure to the toxin is through ingestion of fresh or dry plant materials, consuming improperly prepared sago, or eating meat from animals that have ingested Sago Palm plant materials. Signs of poisoning typically occur within 12 hours of ingestion. Signs include moderate to severe gastrointestinal symptoms (diarrhea, vomiting, etc.). These may be accompanied by weakness, lethargy, seizures, coma, and sometimes death.

Datura spp.

JIMSONWEED, THORNAPPLE, SACRED DATURA

Datura from the Sanskrit word for Thornapple (dhatura).

Solanaceae (Nightshade Family)

DESCRIPTION: *Datura* spp. are large, shrubby annuals or short-lived perennials, reaching about 2 m tall and 1 m wide on average. The coarse leaves are large (15 cm long), triangular, and arranged in an alternating pattern along the stem. Growth habit, leaf shape, and size can vary significantly, based on growing conditions. The large (5–20 cm long), trumpet-shaped flowers are typically white, but can be lavender or purple in some varieties. Fruits are large, spiny balls. *Datura* is distinguished from the closely related *Brugmansia* in part because *Datura* flowers are typically positioned upright and erect, and *Brugmansia* flowers are pendulous. From an ethnobotanical perspective, *Datura* is one of the most fascinating plants, with a nearly worldwide history of uses for both ceremonial and medicinal applications, with numerous anthropological reports of uses dating back to prehistoric times.

DISTRIBUTION AND HABITAT: The origin of *Datura* is disputed. The greatest diversity of *Datura* species is found in Mexico and Central America, which makes this the likely center of origin. However, due to the nearly worldwide distribution of *Datura*, multiple centers of origin may exist. The taxonomy of *Datura* is also disputed, further confused by widespread cultivation and hybridization of *Datura*. Multiple *Datura* species are distributed throughout North America. *Datura* is often found along roadsides, ditches, and other dry, disturbed wasteland.

TOXIC AGENT(S): All parts of the plant should be considered poisonous. The toxic agents include anticholinergic alkaloids, including atropine, hyoscyamine, and scopolamine. These alkaloids can block chemical messages sent by the neurotransmitter acetylcholine. These messages are required for normal function of the body and brain.

SIGNS AND SYMPTOMS OF POISONING: Ingestion of plant parts, inhalation of smoke from burned plant material, or applying plant extracts to skin or mucous membranes may result in poisoning. In fact, there are several reports dating as far back as the 14th and 15th century of "witches" applying *Datura* extracts to broomsticks so they could "fly." Because many of these so-called confessions were obtained under duress, it is impossible to determine the veracity of these claims. However, it is widely reported that *Datura* seeds were used recreationally during the Middle Ages. In more recent cases, poisoning is most often through ingestion. Cases involving chewing and swallowing seeds are particularly likely to result in fatal poisoning. There is typically a rapid onset of symptoms (within 30 minutes) that can last for multiple days. Immediate symptoms may include what is known as the "six Ds of anticholinergic poisoning": dryness of mouth, dysphagia (difficulty swallowing), dysarthria (slurred speech), diplopia (double vision), dry skin, and drowsiness. Death may be caused by respiratory failure or heart arrhythmia.

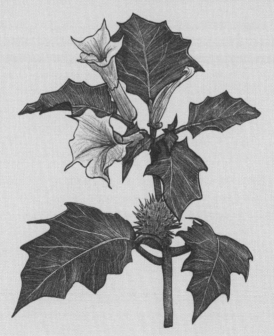

Delphinium spp.

DELPHINIUM, LARKSPUR

Delphinium from the Ancient Greek word for dolphin (delphis).

Ranunculaceae (Buttercup Family)

DESCRIPTION: *Delphinium* spp. are perennial or annual herbaceous flowering plants that range from 30 cm to 120 cm in height. Foliage is lacy, with deeply lobed, sessile leaves arranged in an alternating pattern along the stem. Flowers are bilaterally symmetrical and have a characteristic long nectar spur at the end. Flowers are arranged as a tall and showy spike.

DISTRIBUTION AND HABITAT: There are over 300 species of *Delphinium* with an estimated 60 species found throughout North America. Habitat varies greatly by species, including open fields and prairies to forest and mountainous regions.

TOXIC AGENT(S): All parts of the plant should be considered toxic. *Delphinium* toxicity varies by species and growing conditions. North American species native to mountainous regions are reported to contain the highest levels of toxins. *Delphinium* spp. are known to contain numerous toxic compounds, including multiple diterpenoid alkaloids. The three most toxic of these alkaloids include methyl lycaconitine (MLA), 14-deacetylnudicauline (DAN), and nudicauline. These function by blocking acetylcholine receptors in the muscles and brain, causing neuromuscular paralysis.

SIGNS AND SYMPTOMS OF POISONING: Exposure to toxins is through ingestion of fresh or dry plant material. Death can occur within hours of consumption. Indicators of intoxication may include difficulty breathing, rapid heartbeat, muscle twitches, collapse, and death.

Dermatophyllum secundiflorum

TEXAS MOUNTAIN LAUREL, TEXAS MESCALBEAN, FRIJOLITO, FRIJOLILLO

Dermatophyllum from the Latin word for skin leaf, *secundiflorum* from the Latin words for "flowers on one side."

Fabaceae (Legume Family)

DESCRIPTION: *Dermatophyllum secundiflorum* is a shrub or small tree reaching a maximum height of about 5 m. The leaves are evergreen and pinnately compound, with thick, spoon-shaped leaflets. In spring, the plant has clusters of purple flowers that are described by some as smelling like grape soda. Fruits are 10 cm–long pods containing orange seeds.

DISTRIBUTION AND HABITAT: *Dermatophyllum secundiflorum* is native to southern New Mexico, west Texas, and parts of northern Mexico. A popular ornamental, it has been planted outside of its native range, primarily in the southwestern United States. It tends to be found in rocky limestone soils.

TOXIC AGENT(S): All parts of the plant are toxic, but beans contain the highest concentrations of toxins. Several quinolizidine alkaloids are produced by the plant, but cytisine is the most clinically important. It has a mechanism of toxicity comparable to nicotine, although structurally it is somewhat different. Like nicotine, it is both an agonist and an antagonist at nicotinic receptors and interferes with the regulation of dopamine. It has been used in pharmaceutical smoking-cessation medications with some degree of success.

SIGNS AND SYMPTOMS OF POISONING: Exposure to toxins is through ingestion of fresh or dry plant material and seeds. Ingestion is sometimes intentional due to reported hallucinogenic effects. The plant has emetic properties (meaning that it causes vomiting), and the first signs in poisoning typically include nausea, vomiting, convulsions, and headaches that can last for hours. Hallucinations and "seeing red" have been reported in some cases. Fatalities have been documented in livestock animals and dogs, but no human fatalities were reported in the published medical literature. Clinical signs in fatal cases usually present worsening symptoms, such as weakness, dizziness, twitching, shallow breathing, collapse, and coma. Death is usually due to paralysis of respiratory muscles.

Digitalis spp.

FOXGLOVE

Digitalis from the Latin word for "of the finger."

Plantaginaceae (Plantain Family)

DESCRIPTION: *Digitalis* is a biennial herbaceous plant that grows to about 0.5 m tall, depending on the species. Coarsely textured and often hairy oval leaves alternate along the stem. *Digitalis* is most recognized by showy, bell-shaped flowers that grow in a spike along one side of the flower stalk.

DISTRIBUTION AND HABITAT: *Digitalis* is native to Europe but widely naturalized across most of North America. It is also a commonly cultivated plant in North America. Its native habitat includes open woodlands, roadsides, and fields. It tends to prefer dry to mesic acidic soils.

TOXIC AGENT(S): Sir William Withering, an 18th-century doctor, is largely credited with establishing *Digitalis* as a treatment for congestive heart failure and related ailments. He conducted a systematic study of *Digitalis* as a medicine, and his publication revolutionized how *Digitalis* and other medicinal plants were prepared, dosed, and distributed. Withering did not discover *Digitalis* as a medicinal plant, however. *Digitalis* is one of the most well-known poisonous and medicinal plants and has been used for many centuries in various medicinal applications. In Withering's own account, he describes observing a patient with congestive heart failure and learning of a medicinal tea, including *Digitalis*, that seemed to have a beneficial effect. *Digitalis* was a common feature of the cottage garden and likely employed in various folk remedies long before Withering's publication. All parts of the plant contain toxins, but most reported cases of poisoning are related to some form of consumption of leaf tissue. *Digitalis* produces the cardiac glycoside digoxin that works similarly to other cardiac glycosides by interfering with cell membrane potential. They have historically been used at therapeutic doses to increase the strength of heartbeat contractions while reducing heart rate to create a more efficient cardiac output.

SIGNS AND SYMPTOMS OF POISONING: Although used medicinally for centuries, *Digitalis* has what is referred to as a "narrow therapeutic index," and overdose can quickly result in fatality due to heart failure. There are records of numerous accidental and intentional fatal poisonings caused by *Digitalis*. Signs of overdose may include sweating, light-headedness, slow heartbeat, low blood pressure, and general gastrointestinal disturbances. Death may be caused by respiratory failure or arrhythmias. More recently, it has also been determined that *Digitalis* ingestion over time significantly increases the risk of breast cancer.

Gelsemium sempervirens

YELLOW JESSAMINE, FALSE JASMINE

Gelsemium from the Latin word for "shaped like Jasmine," *sempervirens* from the Latin word for evergreen.

Gelsemiaceae (Gelsemium Family)

DESCRIPTION: *Gelsemium sempervirens* is an evergreen vine with reddish brown stems, reaching up to 6 m in length. The attractive leaves are lanceolate and shiny, ranging from 2 cm to 8 cm in length. Flowers are bright yellow trumpets with a strong fragrance. Flowers are abundant and can be present for several months. Fruits are capsules.

DISTRIBUTION AND HABITAT: *Gelsemium sempervirens* is found in its native range from Virginia to Texas in the United States, as well as parts of Mexico and Central America. Typical habitats are woodlands, thickets, and sometimes along roadsides.

TOXIC AGENT(S): All parts of the plant are toxic, including nectar and sap. Plant extracts contain multiple toxic alkaloids, including gelsemine and gelseminine. In small doses, they activate acetylcholine receptors in the nervous system and skeletal muscles and act as psycho-stimulants, appetite suppressants, and mood enhancers. At toxic doses, they overstimulate receptors, resulting in serious impairment of the nervous and neuromuscular systems. *Gelsemium* tinctures were used to treat headaches and other ailments as late as the 1930s. In a quest to learn just how toxic *Gelsemium* might be, author Sir Arthur Conan Doyle conducted and published his own self-experiments with *Gelsemium* when he was just 19 years old. At the end of his experiments, he concluded that he could have ingested considerably more if not for the inconvenience of "extreme diarrhea."

SIGNS AND SYMPTOMS OF POISONING: Exposure to toxins is through ingestion of fresh or dry plant material. Low doses can result in diarrhea, nausea, muscle spasms, and mild paralysis. Higher doses result in vision impairment, paralysis, and death.

Gossypium spp.

COTTON

Gossypium from the Latin word for cotton (gossypion).

Malvaceae (Mallow Family)

DESCRIPTION: *Gossypium* spp. are perennial shrubs or small trees, though they are more often grown as an annual crop plant. Some species can reach up to 3 m tall. Leaves are lobed and arranged in a spiral pattern along the stem. Flowers tend to be showy, with five petals and ten or more stamens. The fruit is a capsule called a boll, and seeds are covered with fibers that extend outside the capsule.

DISTRIBUTION AND HABITAT: *Gossypium* includes about 50 species, two of which are native to North America. Native species are distributed in Mexico, the West Indies, Central America, and tropical Florida. The native habitat of *Gossypium* varies greatly by species; most *Gossypium* is cultivated and found in agricultural habitats. Cotton is one of the earliest agricultural plants, having been cultivated for the last 7,000 years, and is the most important fiber crop in the world, making up 80% of all natural fibers in production.

TOXIC AGENT(S): The entire plant is covered with small black glands that contain the toxin gossypol. The highest concentration of gossypol is found in the seeds. It has several toxic mechanisms. It binds to iron, causing iron deficiency anemia. It disrupts thyroid metabolism. It impairs the cellular biochemistry involved in the generation of cellular energy, and it decreases the contraction force of the heart. Autopsy results indicate it is hepatotoxic, and it impairs reproductive ability. Several countries explored the use of gossypol as a form of male birth control, but later abandoned the research.

SIGNS AND SYMPTOMS OF POISONING: Exposure to toxins is through ingestion of plant material, cottonseed, and unrefined processed plant products, including cottonseed oil. Poisoning is most common in animals that are fed cottonseed. Poisoning may be chronic or acute. In chronic poisoning, clinical signs include anemia, liver damage, and impaired reproductive ability. Acute poisoning may cause cardiac failure and sudden death.

Helleborus spp.

HELLEBORE, MANY OTHERS BASED ON SPECIES

Unresolved Traditionally thought to be derived from the Greek words for "eaten by deer" (ellos bibrosko), it is now believed to predate the Greek language.

Ranunculaceae (Buttercup Family)

DESCRIPTION: *Helleborus* is a perennial that reaches about 35 cm tall, but height varies by species. It has large, leathery, palmately divided leaves, with many species having tough evergreen leaves. In warmer climates, flowers bloom around December; in cooler climates, they bloom in February to March. Flowers are showy, with five or more white to pink petals and numerous stamens.

DISTRIBUTION AND HABITAT: *Helleborus* spp. are native to mountainous regions of southern and eastern Europe and are now broadly distributed throughout the world due to cultivation. In North America, *Helleborus* spp. can be found cultivated in hardiness zone 5 and above, and some cultivars are known to survive as low as zone 3.

TOXIC AGENT(S): All parts of *Helleborus* are toxic, with roots and sap believed to have the highest concentration of toxins. Like most members of the Buttercup Family, *Helleborus* contains toxic glycosides. One known compound, ranunculin, is highly unstable and breaks down into a toxic, oil-like substance called protoanemonin when the plant is wounded, such as might occur when plant parts are chewed. Protoanemonin has a bitter, acrid taste. It can bind to and inactivate several different proteins and can also transfer small molecules known as alkyl groups to DNA, causing DNA alkylation. Many *Helleborus* also contain another type of toxic glycosides known as bufadienolides, including hellebrin, helleborein, and helleborin. These are believed to have a similar mode of action to other cardiac glycosides but are less well understood and may have additional targets.

SIGNS AND SYMPTOMS OF POISONING: Poisoning may occur through handling the plant or ingesting the plant, though ingestion is more likely to cause serious or fatal poisoning. Handling plant material, such as when collecting seeds, can cause mild to severe irritation. Ingesting any parts of the plant can cause burning of the mucous membranes, oral ulcers, gastrointestinal distress, cardiac and respiratory distress, and possibly death.

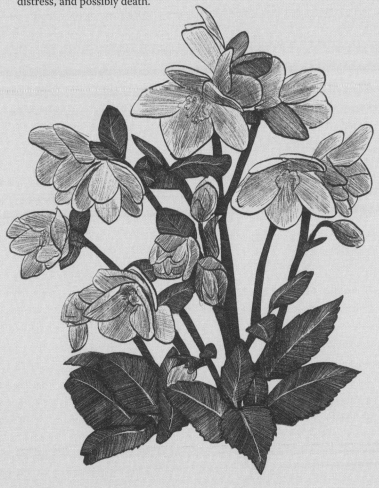

Heracleum mantegazzianum

GIANT HOGWEED

Heracleum is named after Hercules, who is said to have discovered the genus's healing properties, *mantegazzianum* honors Italian anthropologist Paolo Mantegazza (1831–1910).

Apiaceae (Carrot Family)

DESCRIPTION: As the name suggests, Giant Hogweed is a very large perennial, reaching up to 5 m tall in a single growing season. The gargantuan compound leaves are deeply lobed with serrated leaf margins and can grow to be 2 m long. The stem and leaf stalks are hollow and covered with hairs, and often have irregularly shaped, dark purple patches and spots. Flowers are white and clustered into large, umbrella-like structures at the top of the plant.

DISTRIBUTION AND HABITAT: *Heracleum mantegazzianum* is native to Asia and eastern Europe. It was brought to North America in the early 20th century for use as a novelty ornamental plant and is now listed as a noxious invasive plant found throughout large areas of the Pacific Northwest and northeastern North America. Its native habitat is primarily the southern slope of the Caucasus Mountains, but it can colonize a wide array of habitats.

TOXIC AGENT(S): The toxins in *H. mantegazzianum* are primarily the furanocoumarins psoralen, bergapten, and methoxsalen. These damage tissues by binding to DNA molecules when activated by UV light, causing a cascade of cellular damage.

SIGNS AND SYMPTOMS OF POISONING: Skin exposed to sap from *H. mantegazzianum* and UV light may develop severe burns and blisters. Although human deaths due to *H. mantegazzianum* are unlikely, the severity of the tissue damage can be profound, sometimes even requiring surgical interventions and often taking months or even years to fully heal. There are numerous cases requiring hospitalization and long-term treatment due to secondary infections. In rare cases, animals experiencing severe burns have required amputation or euthanasia.

Hippomane mancinella

MANCHINEEL TREE, MANZANILLA DE LA MUERTE

Hippomane from the Greek word for "horse mania," *mancinella* from the Spanish word manzanilla, meaning little apple.

Euphorbiaceae (Spurge Family)

DESCRIPTION: *Hippomane mancinella* is an evergreen tree that grows up to 15 m tall. It has reddish gray bark and simple, alternate leaves. Flowers are inconspicuous. It produces an apple-like fruit—in fact, the English translation of a common name for this tree is "little apple of death."

DISTRIBUTION AND HABITAT: *Hippomane mancinella* is native to tropical regions of North America and is found in Florida, the Bahamas, and Mexico. It is an endangered species in Florida and was nearly intentionally eradicated in much of its native zone due to its toxicity. It can often be found growing among mangroves, along coastal beaches, and near brackish water.

TOXIC AGENT(S): *Hippomane mancinella* contains numerous toxins. The most frequently described include hippomanins, mancinellin, sapogens, and physostigmine. Although the entire plant is toxic, different toxins may be found in different parts of the plant. Most often ingested is physostigmine, found primarily in the fruits. It functions in part by preventing the breakdown of acetylcholine, causing a toxic cholinergic syndrome. It works opposite the way cardiac glycosides like atropine and digitalis function, and in fact physostigmine is used as the antidote to poison from plants like *Digitalis* and *Datura*.

SIGNS AND SYMPTOMS OF POISONING: The toxins can be inhaled, absorbed through the skin, or ingested. Touching any part of the tree should be avoided. Sitting under or near a Manchineel Tree in the rain should be avoided, as several toxins in the Manchineel Tree are water soluble, meaning that they can wash off the tree and onto bystanders. In cases of skin exposure to toxins, severe dermatitis and even blindness may occur. Fruits are reported to have a pleasant smell and taste sweet with the first several bites, quickly changing to a peppery, burning sensation and eventually excruciating pain. Ingestion may cause excessive sweating and salivation, pupil constriction, high blood pressure, and severe gastrointestinal disturbance. Death may occur due to heart paralysis and other effects on respiration and brain function.

Humulus spp.

HOPS

**Origin is uncertain, but is likely derived from the
Proto-Germanic word for hops (humela).**

Cannabaceae (Hemp Family)

DESCRIPTION: *Humulus* is a climbing, perennial vine. Fragrant leaves have toothed edges and 3–5 deep lobes. It is dioecious, meaning individual plants have either male or female flowers. Female flowers are larger and produce the cone-like structure used in beer brewing.

DISTRIBUTION AND HABITAT: *Humulus* spp. have been the topic of taxonomic debate for decades. *Humulus* is distributed throughout the world, with native populations found in North America. Taxonomic confusion arises due to widespread hybridization occurring between native North American varieties and European varieties, often brought to North America for the agricultural production of hops for the growing beer industry, as early as 1629. Wisconsin was the epicenter of American hops production in the 1800s, and by the early 1900s, most hops used in beer production around the world were grown in Wisconsin, California, Oregon, and Washington state. Hops production in Wisconsin and the rest of the Midwest ended in the early 20th century, due to ongoing losses caused by insects and disease.

TOXIC AGENT(S): The exact toxic substances found in *Humulus* are not known. They are believed to be terpenes that give hops their characteristic scent, and a mode of action is not known. It is hypothesized that it may involve the alteration of mitochondrial activity, due to the relatively fast onset of clinical signs after ingestion.

SIGNS AND SYMPTOMS OF POISONING: Although rare, poisoning due to *Humulus* ingestion is on the rise. It is most often observed in dogs (and sometimes cats) who ingest hops used in any form for home brewing; both spent and not spent flowers are toxic. Ingestion may cause a malignant hypothermia involving a dangerously high fever, respiratory distress, clotting disorders, and even death.

Illicium spp.

ANISE, STAR ANISE, ANISE TREE

Illicium **from the Latin word for "to entice" (illicio).**

Schisandraceae (Starvine Family)

DESCRIPTION: *Illicium* is a genus of evergreen woody shrubs or small trees. Leaves are notably aromatic (often described as having a licorice-like fragrance) and arranged in whorls of three to four leaves per node along the stem. Showy flowers are unique and star shaped, and tend to be solitary in most species. Fruits are star-shaped follicles.

DISTRIBUTION AND HABITAT: The *Illicium* genus includes 30 species, two of which are native to North America. North American species are distributed from Florida west to Louisiana. Cultivated varieties can be found throughout the southern half of North America.

TOXIC AGENT(S): Some *Illicium* species are more toxic than others, and different plant parts have varying degrees of toxicity. Toxins of concern include the hydroaromatic compounds safrole and shikimic acid, and the neurotoxin anisatin. Not all *Illicium* species contain each toxin. Safrole is weakly mutagenic and a possible carcinogen. It is also used in the production of illicit drugs like 3,4-Methylenedioxymethamphetamine (ecstasy). The function of shikimic acid is not fully understood. It is bioactive and is used as a precursor molecule in the antiviral medication Tamiflu. Anisatin is a highly toxic neurotoxin that interferes with the function of GABA, a neurotransmitter that blocks the impulses between the nerve cell and the brain. Inhibition of GABA can result in a cascade of consequences, including seizures and death.

SIGNS AND SYMPTOMS OF POISONING: Exposure to toxins is through ingestion of plant tissues, often in the form of a plant tincture or tea. The Food and Drug Administration has advised consumers not to ingest *Illicium* products, specifically products that contain star anise. Several fatalities have been documented in the medical literature, including lethal seed ingestion by children and lethal tea ingestion by adults. Clinical signs of poisoning can occur within hours of ingestion and include vomiting, seizures, frothing at the mouth, and a bluish discoloration of the skin indicating a loss of oxygen in the blood.

Ipomoea spp.

MORNING GLORY

**Ipomoea from the Greek words for worm (ipos)
and resembling (homoios).**

Convolvulaceae (Morning Glory Family)

DESCRIPTION: Morning Glory species are perennial climbing vines. Leaves are typically heart shaped, but this varies by species. Morning Glories produce large, showy, funnel-shaped flowers that range from white to purple.

DISTRIBUTION AND HABITAT: There are at least 30 species of Morning Glory native to North America. Morning Glories are distributed throughout the world, except much of Europe. Habitat varies by species, but they are often found in sunny, disturbed areas.

TOXIC AGENT(S): Morning Glory seeds contain the highest concentration of toxins. The toxic agents in Morning Glory vary by species. Most contain ergine (d-lysergic acid), primarily in the seeds. Ergine concentrations vary considerably by species and environmental conditions. Ergine is a well-known hallucinogen that primarily acts on serotonin receptors to cause a cascade of outcomes, including reduced inhibitions and increased hallucinations (visual imageries). It is believed that the ergine in Morning Glory seeds is produced by *Periglandula*, a symbiotic endophytic fungus, and not the plant. In addition to ergine, some Morning Glory species contain more lethal toxins. For example, Bush Morning Glory (*Ipomoea carnea*), contains swainsonine and calystegines. Swainsonine functions in part by preventing the breakdown of certain small sugar molecules—these molecules build up inside the cell, disrupting normal cell function and potentially killing the cell. The precise mechanism of calystegine toxins is not yet understood, but they are also believed to disrupt cell function.

SIGNS AND SYMPTOMS OF POISONING: Exposure to toxins in humans is almost always the result of ingestion of Morning Glory seeds or seed extracts. The effects of ergine poisoning occur 20–30 minutes after ingestion and may be mild to severe, including nausea, vomiting, rapid heartbeat, visual and auditory hallucinations, and psychosis. Reported deaths from ergine intoxication are usually accidental deaths caused by erratic behavior. Ergine may also cause suicidal ideation. Swainsonine is a cumulative poison—although this could theoretically affect any mammals, it primarily affects livestock animals who have consumed toxic plants over a period of weeks or months.

Jatropha spp.

SPURGE NETTLE, PHYSIC NUT, BLACK VOMIT NUT

Jatropha from the Ancient Greek words for physician and nourishment.

Euphorbiaceae (Spurge Family)

DESCRIPTION: *Jatropha* spp. are typically shrubs or small trees with palmately lobed leaves. *Jatropha* is monoecious, producing separate male and female flowers on the same plant. The stems contain copious amounts of toxic latex when wounded. Female flowers are large and bright pink. They produce a large capsular fruit, which is referenced in several of the common names given to this plant.

DISTRIBUTION AND HABITAT: *Jatropha* spp. are native to the North American tropics, including Mexico and Central America. *Jatropha* is highly adaptable and can be found growing in a wide range of habitats south of hardiness zone 9. Encouraging work exploring the use of *Jatropha* extracts as a biofuel are currently underway, resulting in significant increases in the potential for human exposure as *Jatropha* has become an agricultural crop in some parts of the world.

TOXIC AGENT(S): There are numerous toxic compounds in *Jatropha*. The most lethal is jatrophin, a ricin-like toxin that inactivates the function of ribosomes, effectively stopping protein synthesis and killing cells. It also contains the toxin phorbol which has been shown to promote inflammation and tumor development.

SIGNS AND SYMPTOMS OF POISONING: Any known or suspected ingestion should be considered an urgent medical emergency. The effects of poisoning may take up to ten hours to manifest. Symptoms of intoxication due to ingestion tend to be nonspecific but have been described as the symptoms of "severe food poisoning." Poisoning will ultimately progress to kidney and liver problems, potential seizures, severe dehydration, and death, if left untreated.

Kalmia spp.

Multiple based on species:

SHEEP KILL, SHEEP LAUREL, LAMBKILL, BOG LAUREL, MOUNTAIN LAUREL

Kalmia in honor of Finnish botanist Pehr Kalm (1716–1779).

Ericaceae (Heath Family)

DESCRIPTION: *Kalmia* spp. are small, beautiful shrubs with small, evergreen, leathery, narrow leaves that alternate along the stem. A distinguishing feature of *Kalmia* is the flowers, which are showy and colorful reds, pinks, purples, and whites. Flower petals are fused into a unique bowl-like shape. Anthers sit in small pockets inside the flower, and when a pollinator lands on the flower, anthers pop out and release pollen onto the pollinator.

DISTRIBUTION AND HABITAT: There are 17 *Kalmia* species native to North America. *Kalmia microphylla* is one of the most broadly distributed in North America. It is found in boggy environments, lakeshores, and sometimes other wetlands, from Alaska to California and as far east as Ontario. *Kalmia angustifolia*, colloquially known as Lambkill, is broadly distributed throughout eastern North America, from Quebec, Canada, to Georgia, United States.

TOXIC AGENT(S): Like many plants in the Ericaceae Family, *Kalmia* produces a group of neurotoxins known as grayanotoxins (GTX), also referred to as rhodotoxins and andromedotoxins in older literature. All parts of the plant are known to be toxic. Twenty-five different GTX have been isolated, but GTX I, GTX II, and GTX III are believed to be the most clinically relevant in poisoning cases, all of which have been isolated from *Kalmia*. GTX disrupts the ability of cells to send electrical signals by blocking voltage-gated sodium channels in cell membranes, causing the vagal nervous system to be continually stimulated. This primarily affects heart muscles and the central nervous system.

SIGNS AND SYMPTOMS OF POISONING: Exposure to toxins is primarily via ingestion. A burning sensation in the mouth may be experienced immediately upon consumption of any parts of the *Kalmia* plant. Within 30 minutes to six hours of consumption, poisoning may result in semiparalysis, altered states of consciousness, heart arrhythmias, low blood pressure, and possibly death.

Karwinskia humboldtiana

COYOTILLO, TULLIDORA

Karwinskia honors botanist Baron W. F. von Karvinsky (1780–1855), *humboldtiana* honors German naturalist Baron Alexander von Humboldt (1769–1859).

Rhamnaceae (Buckthorn Family)

DESCRIPTION: *Karwinskia humboldtiana* is a shrub or tree (maximum height about 6 m) with long (up to 20 cm) elliptical to oval leaves. Leaves are attached along the stem in an opposite arrangement. Individual leaves have a prominent opposite (pinnate) venation, with a prominent dot-and-dash pattern on the underside of leaves. Flowers are small and white and form in clusters along the stem. The toxic fruit is berrylike and black at maturity, and contains a pit.

DISTRIBUTION AND HABITAT: *Karwinskia humboldtiana* is native to parts of Texas and Mexico. It is distributed throughout the dry rangeland of southwestern Texas and much of Mexico to Southern California. It is found in a wide range of habitats but preferentially grows in dry, shallow soils.

TOXIC AGENT(S): *Karwinskia humboldtiana* produces four different anthracenone toxins, also referred to as "Buckthorn Toxins." All plant parts contain anthracenone toxins, but the highest concentrations are found in mature fruit. These toxins are believed to cause the loss of the protective fatty layer that surrounds nerve cells. Demyelinated nerve cells have a diminished ability to send electrical impulses, causing muscle weakness and paralysis.

SIGNS AND SYMPTOMS OF POISONING: Exposure to toxins is primarily due to accidental ingestion of berries, most frequently reported in children. Poisoning due to *Karwinskia humboldtiana* consumption can be very difficult to diagnose because symptoms mimic several other chronic conditions. Signs of poisoning may manifest one to ten days after consuming berries, including progressive weakness and paralysis. In severe cases, bulbar palsy and respiratory failure may occur, causing death. Children are the most afflicted. In North America, approximately five human deaths are attributed to *K. humboldtiana* poisoning annually. It is also poisonous to animals; livestock losses due to consumption of berries are known to occur.

Lantana camara

LANTANA

**Lantana refers to *Viburnum lantana*,
camara from the Latin word for having an arched cover, or a vault.**

Verbenaceae (Vervain Family)

DESCRIPTION: *Lantana* is a sprawling or viny perennial shrub, reaching up to 6 m in height. It has simple, ovate, opposite leaves that give off a strong odor when crushed. Flowers are produced in clusters at the tips of the stems. Flowers have four petals and can have many different colors, due to flowers changing color after pollination occurs. The fruit is dark purple and berrylike.

DISTRIBUTION AND HABITAT: *Lantana* is native to Central and South America, although it has been widely used as an ornamental plant and is considered an invasive species in many areas.

TOXIC AGENT(S): All parts of the plant are toxic and contain triterpene acids called lantadene A and lantadene B. These function as hepatatoxins (which are toxic to the liver) and interfere with the flow of bile from the liver. It is often reported in the media that the unripe berries have the highest concentrations of toxins, but this was not corroborated in the scientific literature. Until confusion surrounding the distribution of toxins in *Lantana* is eradicated, it is not advised to eat any plant part or berries.

SIGNS AND SYMPTOMS OF POISONING: Exposure to toxins is through ingestion of fresh or dry plant material. It is primarily toxic to sheep and other grazing livestock animals. It is also toxic to humans, but no human deaths were reported out of over 1,300 cases. Fatalities in dogs are rare but do occur. Clinical signs may be evident within a few hours of consumption. Signs include diarrhea, difficulty breathing, weakness, and loss of appetite. Fatal doses usually result in death within one to three weeks, although extremely high doses can take only two to four days.

Lathyrus odoratus

SWEET PEA

Lathyrus **from the Greek word for very (lathyros),**
odoratus **from the Latin word for fragrant.**

Fabaceae (Legume Family)

DESCRIPTION: *Lathyrus odoratus* is the popular garden Sweet Pea. It is an annual vine, reaching up to 2 m in length on winged stems. Leaves are pinnate, with two leaflets. Forked tendrils near the leaf petioles can attach to support structures and allow the plant to climb. Flowers are large (more than 2 cm) and highly fragrant, with the typical pea-flower morphology including a banner, wings, and keel. It can be found in about every color except yellow. Fruits are hairy, pealike pods, up to 7 cm in length, containing 3–6 seeds.

DISTRIBUTION AND HABITAT: *Lathyrus odoratus* originates from the Mediterranean, where it is a critically endangered species in its native habitat. It is widely planted throughout the world as a popular garden ornamental. A close relative, *Lathyrus latifolius,* is an exotic invasive species distributed throughout North America.

TOXIC AGENT(S): All *Lathyrus* species are reported to have varying degrees of toxicity. *Lathyrus* seeds contain β-aminopropionitrile and β-N-oxalyl-L-α,β-diaminopropionic acid, organic compounds that affect collagen linkage in connective tissues. This can result in bone disorders (osteolathyrism) and aortic aneurysms (angiolathyrism).

SIGNS AND SYMPTOMS OF POISONING: Exposure to toxins is through ingestion of seeds and seed pods. Poisoning tends to be cumulative, and symptoms develop over repeated exposures to seeds and seed pods. Signs of osteolathyrism include bone pain, skeletal deformities, and fatigue. Signs of angiolathyrism include fatigue, shortness of breath, racing heartbeat, chest pain, aneurysm, and death in rare cases.

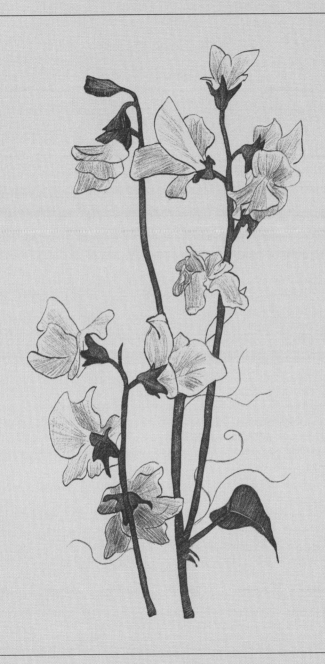

Ligustrum spp.

PRIVET

Ligustrum from the Latin word for privet.

Oleaceae (Olive Family)

DESCRIPTION: *Ligustrum* spp. tend to be densely branched plants, ranging in height from 3 m to 12 m. They have smooth bark, slender twigs, and opposite leaves. Leaves are dark green on the upper surface and pale green on the lower leaf surfaces. Flowers are usually in panicles, with many small four-petaled flowers. The flowers of many species have a strong odor, which some find unpleasant. Fruits are roundish drupes that mature to a purplish black color.

DISTRIBUTION AND HABITAT: *Ligustrum* is a group of about 50 species of deciduous and evergreen shrubs and small trees, with 11 species found in North America. Privets are native to Europe, Africa, and Asia, but have been extensively planted throughout the world as ornamental or landscape plants. They can be found in a variety of habitats, usually near human habitations, and are widely distributed throughout North America, with populations becoming more scattered in western North America. It is an invasive species in some parts of North America.

TOXIC AGENT(S): The berries, leaves, and bark are toxic. Toxins include syringin, a sesquiterpene lactone, and shikimic acid, an intermediary in the production of amino acids found in plants and bacteria. Both are known to be bioactive compounds and are used in the pharmaceutical industry. For example, syringin reduces inflammation and pain, and shikimic acid is a precursor molecule in the antiviral medication Tamiflu. How they function as toxins is not well understood, but it is likely there are synergistic interactions between these molecules and other plant metabolites that can result in poisonings.

SIGNS AND SYMPTOMS OF POISONING: Exposure to toxins is through ingestion of plant material. Human poisonings are relatively rare, due in part to the bitter taste of berries caused by the toxin syringin. Signs of poisoning occur within a few hours of ingestion, and include vomiting, diarrhea, and abdominal pain. In large doses, hypotension and kidney failure can occur. A lethal dose can cause death within 24 hours.

Lilium **spp.**

LILY

Lilium **from the Latin word for lily.**

Liliaceae (Lily Family)

DESCRIPTION: True lilies are herbaceous perennials arising from an underground bulb, with smooth, lanceolate leaves and showy, six-parted flowers. In lilies, the sepals and petals usually appear to be nearly indistinguishable; in these cases, they are referred to as tepals.

DISTRIBUTION AND HABITAT: There are 22 *Lilium* species found in North America, including several nonnative escapees from cultivation. *Lilium* species are widespread throughout North America in a variety of habitats, from prairies to forests.

TOXIC AGENT(S): All parts of the lily plant, including pollen, are toxic to cats. The toxins responsible have not yet been identified, but they are hypothesized to be water soluble, because even chewing on a leaf can cause kidney failure in cats. Lilies were first determined to be toxic to cats when it was noted that instances of acute renal failure in cats was much more likely to occur during certain times of the year—notably the spring, during Easter, when many homes have Easter lilies.

SIGNS AND SYMPTOMS OF POISONING: Exposure to toxins is through ingestion of any plant materials. Cats will show signs of poisoning very quickly after eating plants. Initial signs include vomiting, salivation, and refusal of food. Gastrointestinal distress seems to subside after 4–6 hours, but by this time the toxins have progressed to cause renal failure. Cats in renal failure caused by lily ingestion die in three to seven days.

Lobelia cardinalis

CARDINAL FLOWER

Lobelia in honor of Belgian botanist Matthias L'Obel,
cardinalis from the word (which might either be Latin or
old English) for "having a bright red color," originally in reference
to the color of a Roman Catholic Cardinal's miter and robes.

Campanulaceae (Bellflower Family)

DESCRIPTION: *Lobelia cardinalis* is an herbaceous perennial growing up to 1.2 m in height. Leaves are up to 20 cm long and 5 cm wide, lance to oval in shape, and toothed along the edge. Bright red flowers are produced in a raceme at the top of the plant. Flowers are bilaterally symmetrical, with a three-lobed lower "lip." Fruits are capsules.

DISTRIBUTION AND HABITAT: *Lobelia cardinalis* is widely distributed across the eastern half of the United States and adjacent parts of Canada, as well as the southwestern United States down to Central America. It tends to grow in forested habitats with rich soils, such as along rivers and lakes.

TOXIC AGENT(S): All parts of the plant are toxic. A pyridine alkaloid called lobeline is the primary toxic agent, although other alkaloids have been identified. Lobeline is a neurotoxin that has multiple modes of action. It has a similar toxicity to nicotine, although structurally it is different. Like nicotine, it is both an agonist and an antagonist at nicotinic receptors and interferes with the regulation of dopamine. Lobeline has been employed for some pharmaceutical applications, such as a smoking cessation aid, but the therapeutic index is very narrow, and there is significant risk of accidental poisoning. In 1993, the Food and Drug Administration banned the sale of lobeline as a smoking cessation aid.

SIGNS AND SYMPTOMS OF POISONING: Exposure to toxins is through ingestion of dry or fresh plant materials or plant extracts. There are historical reports of death associated with *Lobelia* ingestion, but only serious poisonings in the medical literature. Clinical signs of poisoning include nausea, vomiting, diarrhea, coughing, dizziness, bradycardia, tachycardia, miosis, tremors, paralysis, coma, and possibly death.

Malus spp.

APPLE, CRABAPPLE

Malus from the Latin word for apple.

Rosaceae (Rose Family)

DESCRIPTION: *Malus* spp. are a group of deciduous shrubs and small trees, including domesticated apple trees and popular ornamental crabapple trees. They tend to be densely branched, with simple, alternate leaves with toothed edges. Flowers are five-parted and are typically white or pink. The fleshy fruit is called a pome; these typically have five interior compartments that contain several seeds.

DISTRIBUTION AND HABITAT: The greatest diversity of *Malus* species can be found in the mountainous regions of Kazakhstan, which is believed to be the primary center of origin for all apples and crabapples. *Malus* includes 30–35 species, and at least three of these are native to North America. Native crabapples are found throughout North America in woodlands, savannas, and thickets. In addition to native species, there are over 7,500 cultivated varieties of *Malus,* many of which have hybridized with native species and have become naturalized across North America.

TOXIC AGENT(S): The seeds of *Malus* species contain amygdalin, a cyanogenic glycoside. For poisoning to occur, seeds need to be crushed or chewed. Upon digestion of amygdalin, cyanide (HCN) is released, which prevents the release of oxygen from hemoglobin, leading to anoxia.

SIGNS AND SYMPTOMS OF POISONING: Exposure to the toxin is through ingestion of seeds. Conversion of amygdalin to HCN occurs during digestion, and amygdalin is only accessible if seeds are macerated. Signs of cyanide poisoning include weakness, dizziness, vertigo, and difficulty breathing, progressing to coma and eventually cardiac arrest. In serious but nonlethal cases, permanent heart, brain, and nerve defects may occur. Could an apple seed kill you? In theory, yes, but it is unlikely. A lethal dose of amygdalin is reported to be 10–100 times the quantity found in the average apple seed.

Melia azedarach

CHINABERRY TREE, PERSIAN LILAC, PRIDE OF INDIA, BEAD TREE

Melia from the Ancient Greek word for ash tree, azedarach from the Ancient Greek word for noble tree.

Meliaceae (Mahogany Family)

DESCRIPTION: *Melia azedarach* is a deciduous tree in the Mahogany Family, commonly reaching 12 m in height, but it can get much larger. It has long (50 cm) compound leaves on long stalks. Leaflets are dark green above and paler below, with serrate margins. The small, fragrant, five-petaled flowers are usually a pale purple color, and they grow in clusters. The fruit is yellowish and about the size of a marble; it tends to persist through the winter, gradually wrinkling and turning white. This tree is commonly used as a timber source, with the wood resembling teak. Cut branches with fruits attached are used in floral arrangements and as outdoor decor.

DISTRIBUTION AND HABITAT: *Melia azedarach* is native to Southeast Asia, from India to Australia, and has been widely planted in suitable climates around the world for its ornamental characteristics and as a source of wood. It is believed to have been introduced to North America as early as the late 1700s or early 1800s, and has since naturalized across Mexico and the southern half of the United States. It can be found along roadsides, disturbed habitats, and forest openings, as well as in more pristine habitats. It is considered an invasive species in some states, although it is still available for sale from many sources.

TOXIC AGENT(S): Several terpenoids, collectively called meliatoxins, can be found in all parts of the plant, but are most concentrated in the seeds and bark. They are enterotoxins and neurotoxins. The mode of action is poorly understood.

SIGNS AND SYMPTOMS OF POISONING: Exposure to toxins is through ingestion. Instances of human poisoning are usually the result of berries being consumed. Clinical signs usually appear relatively quickly after ingestion but may take up to a couple of hours. Initial symptoms are usually gastrointestinal—vomiting, cramping, diarrhea, etc. These can progress to hypersalivation, dizziness, weakness, headache, blurred vision, numbness, and coma. Death is usually the result of respiratory arrest.

Melilotus **spp.**

SWEET CLOVER

Melilotus **from the Greek words for honey (meli)
and legume (lotus).**

Fabaceae (Legume Family)

DESCRIPTION: *Melilotus* species are annual or biennial herbaceous plants reaching up to 2.5 m in height. Trifoliate leaves are arranged alternately and tend to be widely spaced along the stem. Flowers are borne in narrow racemes at the stem tips, composed of small (8 mm long) flowers with five petals, colored white or yellow, depending on the species.

DISTRIBUTION AND HABITAT: Native to Eurasia, *Melilotus* species are now widely distributed throughout North America and the world due to use in agriculture, primarily as a green manure. When escaped from cultivation, it tends to be found in open, grassy habitats, such as meadows and prairies.

TOXIC AGENT(S): *Melilotus* contains coumarin, an organic compound responsible for the smell of hay and cut grass. By itself, coumarin is considered mildly toxic to humans, but not lethal. However, if the clover turns moldy, there are certain kinds of fungi that transform coumarin into dicoumarol, which acts as an anticoagulant in the body. Thus, inhalation or consumption of moldy clover could result in dicoumarol poisoning.

SIGNS AND SYMPTOMS OF POISONING: Exposure to toxins may occur through inhalation or ingestion. Dicoumarol poisoning results in hemorrhaging, and exposure can be chronic or acute. Few signs may be present. Chronic exposure may cause anemia, bloody stools, and nosebleeds. Acute exposure can cause internal and external hemorrhaging and lead to a rapid death with few signs.

Menispermum canadense

MOONSEED

Menispermum canadense **from the Greek words for moon (meni)
and seed (spermum),** *canadense* **from Canada.**

Menispermaceae (Moonseed Family)

DESCRIPTION: *Menispermum canadense* is a deciduous, dioecious, woody vine. Leaves are palmately lobed with 3–7 lobes, and peltate (petiole attached to the underside of the leaf, rather than the edge). Inconspicuous male flowers dry up soon after flowering. Small, white female flowers produce grape-like fruits (drupes). Fruits contain crescent-shaped seeds; hence the name Moonseed. The crescent-shaped seed is also a characteristic that is useful in helping to distinguish Moonseed from edible species like wild grape, *Vitas.*

DISTRIBUTION AND HABITAT: Moonseed is distributed throughout eastern North America, growing in woods and thickets, and along streams, bluffs, and rocky hillsides.

TOXIC AGENT(S): All parts of the plant contain multiple toxic alkaloids, including berberine, menispine, menispermine, and dauricine. The most lethal of these is dauricine, an alkaloid which interferes with electrical signals that regulate heartbeat.

SIGNS AND SYMPTOMS OF POISONING: Exposure to toxins is through ingestion of any plant material. Most frequently, poisonings are caused by misidentification of Moonseed as an edible wild grape. There are cases of children dying due to accidental ingestion of the fruits. Signs of poisoning can occur very quickly after ingestion. Convulsions are the primary clinical sign attributed to Moonseed poisoning.

Nerium oleander

COMMON OLEANDER

Nerium from the Greek word for fresh water (neros).
The derivation of *oleander* is not entirely resolved.
One theory is that it is derived from Latin names for the plant.
Another theory is that it is derived from the Greek
words for "I kill man" (ollyo andras).

Apocynaceae (Dogbane Family)

DESCRIPTION: *Nerium oleander* is an evergreen shrub, reaching maximum heights of about 4 meters. Long (8–12 cm), narrow leaves are arranged in whorls along the woody stem. Showy flowers are produced at the end of the stems. Purple, pink, or white flowers are large (about 3 cm across), with five fused petals. The Oleander flower also has many interesting traditions and folklore associated with it. In Greek mythology, Oleander represents everlasting love, referencing the star-crossed lovers Leander and Hero. Galveston, Texas, is popularly known as "Oleander City," after the shrub was planted throughout the island following a devastating hurricane that struck in 1900. Local Galveston lore claims it was the work of pirate Jean Lafitte's gardener: Ole Anderson.

DISTRIBUTION AND HABITAT: *Nerium oleander* is native to the Mediterranean region, Iran, India, and parts of China. It has been extensively cultivated across tropical and subtropical regions of the world for centuries. It is considered an invasive, noxious weed in Death Valley National Park in California and Lake Mead National Park in Nevada. It is also considered invasive throughout Florida. In its native habit, it can be found along rocky streambeds and riverbanks. As a widely cultivated ornamental, relic plantings can be found in many different habitats.

TOXIC AGENT(S): All plant parts are toxic, and multiple lethal toxins have been isolated from *Nerium oleander*. The most harmful of these include the cardiac glycosides (cardenolides), oleandrin, and oleandrigenin. These toxins disrupt the ability of heart muscle cells to beat in a rhythmic pattern by interfering with cell membrane potential.

SIGNS AND SYMPTOMS OF POISONING: THERE IS NO SAFE LEVEL OF CONSUMPTION. Effects of poisoning will typically occur within two hours of ingestion. Signs may include ulcers on the mucous membranes of the mouth, gastrointestinal distress, and a low, irregular heartbeat. Poisoning may result in heart failure and death. Any suspected ingestion should be considered a medical emergency.

Nicotiana spp.

TOBACCO

**Nicotiana in honor of Jean Nicot, a 16th-century scholar
who first brought tobacco to France.**

Solanaceae (Nightshade Family)

DESCRIPTION: *Nicotiana* spp. in North America are primarily annual and perennial herbs, most reaching 1–2 m tall, depending on the species. A handful of *Nicotiana* species are shrubs or small trees, reaching about 3 m tall. A showy, tubular flower with five petals is characteristic of the genus. Flowers are white in most species, but may be found in a variety of colors, particularly those cultivars that have been developed as ornamental plants. The entire plant is typically slightly hairy and somewhat sticky.

DISTRIBUTION AND HABITAT: *Nicotiana* is native to North and South America. There are at least 12 *Nicotiana* species native to North America, broadly distributed from Canada to Mexico. *Nicotiana* is also grown in large-scale commercial production for tobacco leaves across North America.

TOXIC AGENT(S): The primary toxins in *Nicotiana* include anabasine and nicotine. Different species and different plant parts will have varying concentrations of toxins. Nicotine and related toxins are primarily found in the roots, where they are produced, and in the leaves, where they are stored to serve as plant defense molecules. They also have a similar mode of action in the human body. In small doses, they activate acetylcholine receptors in the nervous system and skeletal muscle and act as psychostimulants, appetite suppressants, and mood enhancers. At toxic doses, they overstimulate receptors, resulting in serious impairment of the nervous and neuromuscular systems. Nicotine is highly toxic, but surprisingly, the lethal dose of nicotine is unknown. It is frequently reported to be 60 mg for an average adult male; however, this value appears to be based on the results of a scientist's self-experiment with nicotine that was published more than 100 years ago. Even assuming 60 mg is a toxic dose, it is unlikely a typical smoker could ingest a lethal dose. A tobacco cigarette contains 10–20 mg of nicotine, but only about 1.5 mg of this nicotine is delivered via inhalation. Theoretically, it would require smoking about 40 cigarettes within one or two hours to receive a lethal dose.

SIGNS AND SYMPTOMS OF POISONING: Exposure to toxins may occur through inhalation of burned, dried leaves or ingestion of plant material. *Nicotiana* toxicity is more likely to occur in livestock animals than people, although signs and symptoms will be similar. They may include a loss of coordination, muscle twitches and trembling, gastrointestinal distress, and death due to respiratory paralysis.

Oplopanax horridus

DEVIL'S CLUB, DEVIL'S WALKING STICK

Oplopanax from the Ancient Greek words for weapon (hoplon) and cure-all (pan akos), *horridus* from the Latin word for bristly.

Araliaceae (Ginseng Family)

DESCRIPTION: *Oplopanax horridus* is a deciduous, perennial shrub that reaches 3 m high at maturity. The entire plant is covered with sharp, yellow spines up to 2 cm long. Leaves are large (more than 20 cm wide) and attractive, with a palmate shape, somewhat like a maple leaf. They are attached on long petioles in a spiral around the stout, spine-covered stem. Dense clusters of small white flowers mature into numerous red berries. *Oplopanax horridus* has numerous spiritual, medicinal, and practical uses by indigenous people of the Pacific Northwest. Some medicinal applications include treatments for gonorrhea, pain relief, and cold or cough, among others. Some practical, historical uses included using the soft wood for carving fish lures and the berries and charcoal for dye and face paints.

DISTRIBUTION AND HABITAT: *Oplopanax horridus* is native to the Pacific Northwest, where it is primarily found in the temperate rain forests. It is always found in disjunct populations on islands in Lake Superior.

TOXIC AGENT(S): Despite being greatly important to indigenous groups across a large area of the Pacific Northwest, limited pharmacological assessment has been completed specifically for *O. horridus*. Berries are reported to be highly toxic to humans, but no assessment of these toxins has been reported in the literature; however, historical use of berries as an emetic and purgative supports the claims of toxicity. Evaluation of root tissues has identified several compounds that have a cytotoxic effect on cancer cells and may act by disrupting cell division.

SIGNS AND SYMPTOMS OF POISONING: Exposure to toxins may occur through plant extract contact with skin and mucous membranes or through ingestion. Skin contact can cause severe dermatitis. The consequences of ingestion are largely unknown. Documented folk medicine and traditional applications suggest poisoning could result in severe hypoglycemia, nausea, and other gastrointestinal disturbances.

Phoradendron spp.

AMERICAN MISTLETOE

**Phoradendron from the Latin words for thief (phora)
and tree (dendron).**

Santalaceae (Sandalwood Family)

DESCRIPTION: *Phoradendron* species are hemiparasitic woody shrubs, meaning they rely on their host plant for only some of their nutrition. *Phoradendron* parasitize many different host tree species. They rely on their host trees for minerals and water, using a haustorium, which is a rootlike structure that penetrates tree tissues. Some *Phoradendron* species have large, photosynthetic leaves, while others have inconspicuous leaves. Flowers are small and inconspicuous, with no petals and 3–4 greenish sepals. The fruit is a berry that can be white, yellow, orange, or red, with a sticky juice inside containing one to several seeds. Some *Phoradendron* are host specific; others are generalists and can infect several different species. Trees that have been parasitized will often have branches that are swollen and distorted in some manner, forming burls or witches' brooms. Parasitized trees are often more susceptible to insect attack, and therefore may show signs of insect damage or stress.

DISTRIBUTION AND HABITAT: The *Phoradendron* genus includes 244 species of Mistletoe, seven of which can be found in North America. Mistletoe is distributed throughout Central America and Mexico, the southern United States, and along the Pacific and Atlantic coasts of the United States. They are found where their host plants grow.

TOXIC AGENT(S): The toxicity of *Phoradendron* is not fully understood, and may be influenced by the host species or which part of the plant is consumed, and at what time of the year. Potentially toxic compounds have been discovered, including glycoprotein lectins, phoratoxins, and phenylethylamino compounds, the latter two of which have cardiac effects. Although not explored in the literature, it is possible that *Phoradendron* toxicity may be influenced by the host species.

SIGNS AND SYMPTOMS OF POISONING: Exposure to toxins is through ingestion of plant materials, particularly berries or plant extracts in teas or elixirs. In the reported cases of people accidentally or otherwise consuming *Phoradendron*, many were asymptomatic. Those experiencing symptoms reported the following: gastrointestinal upsets, drowsiness, ataxia, and seizures. However, at least one death has been reported in the recent literature, from an individual that brewed and consumed an elixir using an unknown quantity of *Phoradendron*.

Phytolacca **spp.**

POKEWEED, POKEBERRY, INKBERRY

**Phyto from the Greek word for plant,
lacca from the Latin word for red dye.**

Phytolaccaceae (Pokeweed Family)

DESCRIPTION: *Phytolacca* spp. may be deciduous or evergreen, growing from 1 m to 25 m in height. They have large, simple alternate leaves that are ovate to elliptical in shape and have smooth leaf margins. Flowers are borne in large racemes at the tips of branches. They typically have five sepals that are greenish, whitish, or pinkish in color. They are followed by green berries that ripen to a purple-black color that contain a reddish-colored juice. The juice was historically used as an ink; hence the common name Inkberry. The juice will also stain the skin.

DISTRIBUTION AND HABITAT: *Phytolacca* includes about 25 species of perennial shrubs and trees, with six species found in North America. There is one native species in North America, widely distributed outside of the northern Great Plains and Rocky Mountain states. The remaining species found in North America are nonnative and usually found as cultivated plants, or escapees from cultivation, in widely scattered or isolated locations throughout North America.

TOXIC AGENT(S): All parts of the plant are toxic, with the highest concentration of toxins found in the roots. A variety of bioactive compounds have been isolated from the plant, with the most toxic being phytolaccine (an alkaloid), which acts as a gastrointestinal irritant and can cause severe hemorrhagic gastritis. It also contains small, bioactive compounds known as mitogens that stimulate cell division and may disrupt the cell cycle. Saponins are also found in high concentration and may contribute to gastrointestinal distress.

SIGNS AND SYMPTOMS OF POISONING: Most cases of human poisoning are related to the consumption of improperly prepared plant leaves for a regional dish known as "poke sallet," or ingestion of berries. Signs of poisoning always include severe gastrointestinal distress (including vomiting and bloody diarrhea), thirstiness, dizziness, drowsiness, drop in blood pressure, rapid heart rate, and seizures. Death is usually due to respiratory failure, and one reported case indicated death occurred within 45 minutes of consuming raw leaves.

Podophyllum peltatum

MAYAPPLE

**Podophyllum from the Greek words for foot (podo) and leaf
(phylum), *peltatum* from the Latin word for shield shaped (pelta).**

Berberidaceae (Barberry Family)

DESCRIPTION: *Podophyllum peltatum* is an herbaceous perennial
with large, umbrella-like leaves. Each plant has two palmately lobed
leaves and one flower stalk. Flowers are large (3–5 cm across) with 6–9
white petals and numerous stamens. Each plant has a single fruit that is
yellow and egg shaped at maturity.

DISTRIBUTION AND HABITAT: *Podophyllum peltatum* is native
to eastern Canada and throughout the Midwest and eastern United
States. It can be found in shady, moist woodlands.

TOXIC AGENT(S): All parts of the plant may contain toxins, but
the highest concentrations are found in the root, rhizome, fruit, and
seed. The primary toxic agent in *Podophyllum peltatum* is podophyllin.
The precise mode of action of podophyllin is not understood, but it is
believed to function as an antimitotic, preventing cell division by stopping mitosis. Podophyllin is also reported to be cytotoxic (causing cell
death) and a possible teratogen (causing defects in a developing embryo).

SIGNS AND SYMPTOMS OF POISONING: Exposure to toxins may occur externally through plant extract contact with skin and
mucous membranes, or through ingestion of plant materials. Mayapple
extracts have been used as both a folk remedy and prescribed medicine
for the treatment of warts. It is also the basis for several anticancer drugs,
including Etoposide, a chemotherapeutic agent used to treat lung cancer,
ovarian cancer, testicular cancer, leukemia, and neuroblastoma. Despite
its medicinal applications, external or internal use of plant extracts
results in chronic or acute poisoning. The teratogenic effects of Mayapple

are not well studied, and pregnant women should avoid all exposure to Mayapple. Ingestion of large quantities of Mayapples or Mayapple extracts will cause gastrointestinal distress, confusion, weakness or numbness in the extremities, and possibly multisystem organ failure.

Prunus spp.

CHERRY, CHOKECHERRY, PLUM, APRICOT, PEACH, ALMOND

Prunus from the Latin word for plum tree.

Rosaceae (Rose Family)

DESCRIPTION: This group of shrubs and trees includes many widely consumed fruits, including cherries, peaches, plums, nectarines, apricots, and almonds. A common characteristic is the fruits, called drupes, which are fleshy fruits with a single, hard seed at the center, commonly called the "stone" or "pit." Most *Prunus* spp. have simple, alternate, lance-shaped leaves and five-petaled white or pink flowers.

DISTRIBUTION AND HABITAT: *Prunus* species can be found widely distributed throughout North America.

TOXIC AGENT(S): The seeds and leaves of *Prunus* species contain several cyanogenic glycosides, including prunasin, prulaurasin, and amygdalin. For poisoning to occur, seed and leaf tissues need to be crushed or chewed. Upon digestion of cyanogenic glycosides, cyanide (HCN) is produced, which prevents the release of oxygen from hemoglobin, leading to anoxia.

SIGNS AND SYMPTOMS OF POISONING: Exposure to toxins is through ingestion of seeds and leaves. Conversion of cyanogenic glycosides to HCN occurs during digestion, and these are only accessible if seeds and tissues are macerated. Signs of cyanide poisoning include weakness, dizziness, vertigo, and difficulty breathing, progressing to coma and eventually cardiac arrest. In serious but nonlethal cases, permanent heart, brain, and nerve defects may occur. Could eating *Prunus* leaves or seeds really kill you? Unequivocally, yes, some species of *Prunus* contain very high levels of cyanogenic glycosides in leaf tissues and seeds and are unsafe for consumption by humans, pets, or livestock. For example, there are published cases of life-threatening accidental poisonings in humans from consumption of the Chokecherry (*Prunus virginiana*) pulp. There are also published reports of Chokecherry consumption causing the death of several moose calves and livestock animals. In these cases, ruminant animals are more susceptible to fatal poisoning. Another example is Bitter Almond, *Prunus amygdalus* var. amara, with multiple reports of life-threatening or fatal poisonings in humans.

Pulsatilla spp.

PASQUE FLOWER, WIND FLOWER, PRAIRIE CROCUS

Unresolved Suggested *Pulsatilla* from the Latin word for knocking/beating/keeping time (pulsa).

Ranunculaceae (Buttercup Family)

DESCRIPTION: *Pulsatilla* spp. are herbaceous perennials, characterized by finely dissected, lacelike leaves. Flowers are bell shaped and produce plumed seed heads. They typically bloom in early spring.

DISTRIBUTION AND HABITAT: There are 100 species of *Pulsatilla* distributed worldwide and 25 species native to North America. They are primarily found in cooler regions, in open, prairie-type habitats, and widely distributed throughout the northern half of North America, as well as farther south along the Pacific coast and Rocky Mountains.

TOXIC AGENT(S): Like all plants in the Buttercup Family, *Pulsatilla* spp. contain the glucoside ranunculin in all parts of the plant. Ranunculin is highly unstable and breaks down into a toxic, oil-like substance called protoanemonin when the plant is wounded, such as might occur when plant parts are chewed. Protoanemonin has a bitter, acrid taste. It can bind to and inactivate several different proteins and can also transfer small molecules known as alkyl groups to DNA, causing DNA alkylation.

SIGNS AND SYMPTOMS OF POISONING: Exposure to toxins is primarily via ingestion. Consumption may cause severe gastrointestinal distress, abdominal pain, diarrhea, and nausea. Some cases additionally report severe headaches and dizziness following consumption. Mouth blisters are often reported in livestock and humans that have consumed large quantities. Death may occur due to respiratory failure and cardiac arrest.

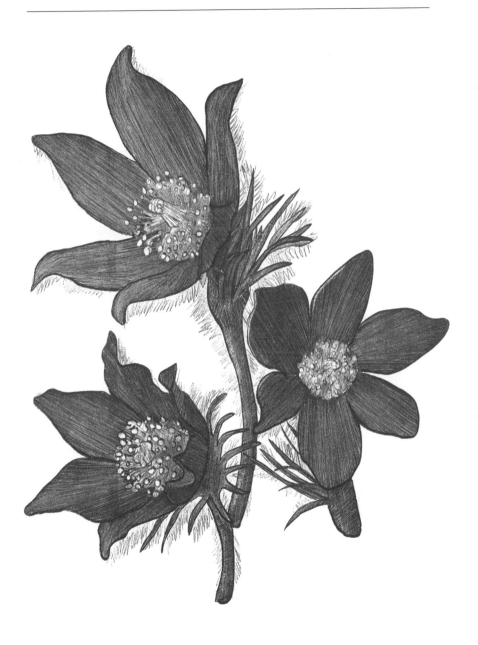

Ranunculus spp.

BUTTERCUP

Ranunculus from the Latin word for tadpole or little frog.

Ranunculaceae (Buttercup Family)

DESCRIPTION: Buttercups are primarily known and named for their shiny yellow flowers. Flowers tend to be simple, with five petals and multiple stamens, although some wild species have white flowers, and there are cultivated varieties with doubled flowers. Buttercups are the only plants with flowers that have a special thin film under the first layer of petal cells to reflect light in a mirrorlike manner. This reflection creates the buttery, glossy appearance of the Buttercup flower. It is hypothesized that this reflective surface may attract pollinators, or it may help to serve as a little space heater. On cooler, overcast days, the flowers can reflect light back into themselves and warm up the plant's reproductive structures.

DISTRIBUTION AND HABITAT: There is still considerable disagreement among plant scientists about the classification of plants in the Buttercup Family, with many species having unresolved taxonomic problems. *Ranunculus* is a large genus in this family, including over 600 species worldwide and 75–80 species in North America. Buttercups are distributed across North America, often preferring damp soil in meadows, pastures, and woodlands. There are also aquatic species that are primarily found in wetlands.

TOXIC AGENT(S): All *Ranunculus* species are poisonous, but concentrations vary significantly between different species. Environmental conditions and time of year also influence toxin concentrations, with the early flowering stage reported to be the most toxic. The toxic agent in Buttercups begins as a glucose-based compound called ranunculin. This compound is highly unstable and breaks down into a toxic, oil-like substance called protoanemonin when the plant is wounded, such as might occur when plant parts are chewed. It can bind to and inactivate several different proteins and transfer small molecules known as alkyl groups to DNA, causing DNA alkylation. Alkylated DNA causes mutations, disrupts cell division, and ultimately kills the cells.

SIGNS AND SYMPTOMS OF POISONING: Exposure to toxins is primarily via ingestion. Consumption may cause severe gastrointestinal distress, abdominal pain, diarrhea, and nausea. Some cases additionally report severe headaches and dizziness following consumption. Mouth blisters are often reported in livestock and humans that have consumed large quantities. Death may occur due to respiratory failure and cardiac arrest.

Rhododendron spp.

AZALEA

Rhododendron from the Ancient Greek words or rose (rhodon) and tree (dendro).

Ericaceae (Heath Family)

DESCRIPTION: Azaleas are low shrubs characterized by beautiful, leathery foliage and showy flowers that come in whites, pinks, reds, and oranges. Native species have a large, tubular flower, 5–7 cm long, with stamens that extend outside the flower. Most native Azalea species are deciduous. There is a great variety of flower morphologies of the cultivated Azalea, though they are typically showy and funnel shaped. Flowers may also be doubled or in other configurations, such as long, spidery petals. Cultivated Azaleas may have deciduous or evergreen leaves.

DISTRIBUTION AND HABITAT: There are 17 species of Azalea native to North America and over 10,000 cultivated varieties. In North America, native Azalea species are primarily found in the eastern United States, from Maine to Florida. There is one species native to Canada and one species native to Mexico. Azaleas can be found in a variety of habitats, the most common being woodlands with well-drained, acidic soil.

TOXIC AGENT(S): All Azalea species contain neurotoxins called grayanotoxins (GTX), sometimes called rhodotoxin or andromedotoxins. The specific GTX produced and GTX concentrations vary by species. GTX is present in all parts of the plant, including the pollen. These toxins function in part by disrupting sodium-ion channels in cell membranes, causing the vagal nervous system to be continually stimulated. This primarily affects heart muscles and the central nervous system. Some cultures intentionally harvest honey obtained exclusively from *Rhododendron* called "mad honey." This honey contains high concentrations of grayanotoxin and is used recreationally and ritually. Mad honey production primarily occurs in the Black Sea region of Turkey, where it has been used for thousands of years. There is even reported use of mad honey as a bioweapon. In 67 BCE, King Mithridates the Great ("The Poison King") left pots filled with mad honey in the path of the enemy Roman troops. When the Roman troops were adequately intoxicated, his army returned to slaughter them.

SIGNS AND SYMPTOMS OF POISONING: Exposure to toxins may occur through smoke inhalation of dried plant products, ingestion of plant material, or, most frequently, by intentionally eating honey produced from the Azalea flowers. Signs of intoxication may become apparent 20–30 minutes after consumption and can last for several days. These signs may include sweating, vomiting, altered states of consciousness, heart arrhythmias, low blood pressure, semiparalysis, and possibly death.

Ricinus communis

CASTOR BEAN

Ricinus from the Latin word for tick,
communis from the Latin word for common.

Euphorbiaceae (Spurge Family)

DESCRIPTION: *Ricinus communis* is a fast-growing shrub that can reach over 10 m high in the wild. In cultivation, it grows to about 3 m tall. It has large, star-shaped leaves with up to 12 deep lobes per leaf. Leaves may be up to 1 m long. It produces separate male and female flowers, with the small white male flowers growing directly below the terminal, red female flowers. A spiny red fruit is formed after pollination.

DISTRIBUTION AND HABITAT: *Ricinus communis* is most likely native to tropical regions of eastern Africa but can be found in naturalized populations around the world. In North America, *R. communis* is considered an invasive exotic species in California and Florida. Naturalized populations exist throughout subtropical regions of North America, primarily in disturbed areas such as fields and roadsides.

TOXIC AGENT(S): All plant parts are considered poisonous, but the highest concentration of toxins is contained in seeds. *Ricinus communis* produces ricin. It is regarded as one of the most toxic plants on Earth, and ricin is a category B bioterrorism agent. Ricin is in a category of toxins called toxalbumins—toxic proteins. When ingested, ricin inactivates the function of ribosomes, effectively stopping protein synthesis and killing cells, leading to a cascade of tissue damage and multisystem organ failure.

SIGNS AND SYMPTOMS OF POISONING: THERE IS NO SAFE LEVEL OF CONSUMPTION. Exposure may occur through inhalation or ingestion, though poisoning via ingestion requires the seed coat to be damaged in some manner. A reported route of poisoning is via jewelry made from *R. communis* seeds; in this process, seeds are punctured, and the risk of poisoning increases. Any known or suspected ingestion should be considered an urgent medical emergency. The effects of poisoning may take ten hours or more to manifest. Symptoms of ricin intoxication due to ingestion tend to be nonspecific but have been described as the symptoms of "severe food poisoning." Poisoning will ultimately progress to kidney and liver problems, potentially seizures, severe dehydration, and death, if left untreated.

Robinia spp.

BLACK LOCUST, FALSE ACACIA

Robinia for royal French gardeners Jean and Vespasien Robin.

Fabaceae (Legume Family)

DESCRIPTION: *Robinia* spp. are deciduous shrubs and trees ranging in height from 4 m to 25 m. Leaves are pinnate and composed of 7–21 oval-shaped leaflets. New shoots and young twigs often have thorns or sticky hairs. Flowers are usually in hanging (pendulous) racemes, colored white or pink, usually fragrant, and shaped like pea flowers. Seed pods are brown and resemble flattened pea pods.

DISTRIBUTION AND HABITAT: *Robinia* includes a group of four to ten species native to North America. Native ranges of *Robinia* species in North America include the Desert Southwest, eastern, and southeastern United States. Many have been widely planted outside of their native ranges as landscape trees and have naturalized in those areas. Thus, they can be found in a variety of habitats, such as woodlands and woodland edges, fence rows, along roadsides and other waste areas, and in urban settings.

TOXIC AGENT(S): All parts of the plant are considered toxic, except the flowers. Several potential bioactive compounds have been identified, although their individual toxicity has not yet been determined. A toxalbumin called robin and a lectin called robinin are among those thought to be toxic. They interfere with ribosome function, preventing protein synthesis in the cells.

SIGNS AND SYMPTOMS OF POISONING: Exposure to toxins is primarily through consumption of plant parts, particularly seed pods. Death is rare and seems most likely to occur in equine species. Signs of poisoning may include lack of appetite, diarrhea, vomiting, weakness, dilated pupils, colic, and occasionally death.

Sanguinaria canadensis

BLOODROOT, CANADA PUCCOON

Sanguinaria from the Latin word for bloody, canadensis for Canadian.

Papaveraceae (Poppy Family)

DESCRIPTION: *Sanguinaria canadensis* is a perennial spring ephemeral that reaches up to 50 cm in height. It has a single, rounded leaf that has 5–7 lobes. Solitary white flowers are on a separate stalk, with 8–12 petals and numerous yellow stamens. The leaf and flower stalk emerge from an underground rhizome that contains a bright, orange, caustic sap, which is referenced in the common name "Bloodroot." Fruits are pods. Seeds have special nutrient-dense attachments called eliasomes that strategically function as a food source for ants, providing a mode of seed dispersal.

DISTRIBUTION AND HABITAT: *Sanguinaria canadensis* is native to eastern North America and is distributed from Florida to Nova Scotia and west to the Rocky Mountains. Its preferred habitats are nutrient-rich, deciduous woodlands and floodplains.

TOXIC AGENT(S): All parts of the plant are toxic, but toxin concentration and type vary in different parts of the plant. The primary toxins are the alkaloids sanguinarine and dihydrosanguinarine, which are found in the seeds. Other parts of the plant contain several other alkaloids, some with properties much like opium. Sanguinarine and dihydrosanguinarine cause cell death through the interference of enzymes involved in the transport of vital molecules across cell membranes.

SIGNS AND SYMPTOMS OF POISONING: Exposure to toxins can occur externally through skin and mucous membranes, or internally through ingestion of plant materials or extracts. External exposure to the caustic sap is not life-threatening but can cause necrosis of the skin and underlying tissues, leading to a thick scab called an eschar. Ingestion of seeds or seed oil leads to a condition called epidemic dropsy. Clinical signs include swelling in extremities due to fluid buildup, headache, nausea, diarrhea, erythema, shortness of breath, and glaucoma. About 5% of cases end in mortality, usually due to heart or kidney failure, pneumonia, or respiratory distress.

Senecio spp.

SENECIO, GROUNDSEL, RAGWORT, BUTTERWEED

Senecio from the Latin word for older man.

Asteraceae (Aster Family)

DESCRIPTION: *Senecio* species have alternate leaves and yellow, daisy-like flower heads. An identifying characteristic of *Senecio* is the greenish bracts at the base of each flower head. They do not overlap, like most other species, but merely touch each other on their sides, looking somewhat like a picket fence.

DISTRIBUTION AND HABITAT: *Senecio* is a large and diverse genus, including at least 1,000 species, with 55 species in North America. It is found widely distributed throughout North America, in a variety of open habitats, such as meadows, pastures, and weedy, disturbed areas.

TOXIC AGENT(S): All *Senecio* spp. contain pyrrolizidine alkaloids, with some species more toxic than others. The alkaloids are found in all parts of the plant. When these alkaloids are metabolized in the liver, they are converted to highly reactive pyrroles that cause cellular dysfunction, disrupt cell division, and kill cells. There are multiple reported cases of large-scale human fatalities due to acute poisoning by pyrrolizidine alkaloids. The poisoning can be cumulative, and over time lead to irreversible liver failure.

SIGNS AND SYMPTOMS OF POISONING: Exposure to toxins is through ingestion of fresh or dry plant materials. *Senecio* poisoning is much more common in livestock than people. Poisoning can be chronic or acute. Chronic cases involve repeated low-dose exposures of toxins over several weeks. In these cases, liver tissues are repeatedly injured and healed, and the microscopic veins of the liver become clogged or destroyed, preventing blood flow into and out of the small blood vessels in the liver. In the early stages of chronic poisoning, there may be no symptoms. Once liver function is sufficiently compromised, clinical signs will include fluid buildup in the abdomen (ascites), jaundice, cirrhosis, and liver failure. Acute cases may present with more immediate signs, including a rapid onset of massive ascites and more severe liver damage.

Senegalia berlandieri

GUAJILLO

Senegalia refers to the country of Senegal, *berlandieri* honors French-Mexican naturalist Jean-Louis Berlandier (1805–1851).

Fabaceae (Legume Family)

DESCRIPTION: *Senegalia berlandieri* is a woody shrub with bipinnately compound leaves. Individual leaflets are short (less than 1 cm) and narrow. Approximately 30–50 pairs of leaflets make up a leaf. Flowers are white balls with numerous stamens and no petals. Seeds are contained in long, flat pods.

DISTRIBUTION AND HABITAT: *Senegalia berlandieri* is native to Texas and northeastern Mexico. It can be found growing along hillsides and other dry, sloped terrain.

TOXIC AGENT(S): The published literature describing *S. berlandieri* toxins is surprisingly controversial. One team of scientists reported finding more than 40 alkaloids and other bioactive molecules, including nicotine, nornicotine, mescaline, mimosine, and four amphetamines never previously associated with natural products. It was later marketed and sold as a health food supplement and energy drink, claiming it could increase metabolism and was stronger than ephedrine! However, some scientists responded to the research with a good degree of skepticism, claiming they were likely the result of contaminated labware. To this date, no researchers have been able to confirm the findings from the original lab. Other literature suggests that molecules known as biogenic amines (Bas) contribute to the toxicity of *S. berlandieri*. Overconsumption of Bas can cause a cascade of problems, including the release of adrenaline and noradrenaline and the production of carcinogenic metabolic by-products.

SIGNS AND SYMPTOMS OF POISONING: Exposure to toxins is through consumption of fresh or dry plant material. There are no known reports of human death due to ingestion of *S. berlandieri*, but it is a known poisonous plant for sheep, goats, and, less frequently, cattle. Animals that are allowed to browse *S. berlandieri* for extended periods of time may develop rubbery, uncoordinated legs, known as "guajillo wobbles." In some animals, this progresses to a refusal to move and eventually death.

Senna spp.

SENNA, PISS-A-BED, COFFEE SENNA, OTHERS

Senna **from the Latinized Arabic word for thorny bush.**

Fabaceae (Legume Family)

DESCRIPTION: *Senna* is a large genus that represents a variety of growth habits, including herbs, shrubs, and small trees. Leaves of *Senna* are feathery, with pinnately compound, opposite-paired leaflets. Flowers are white or yellow and arranged on the ends of branches in racemes. Fruits are pods.

DISTRIBUTION AND HABITAT: There are about 250 *Senna* species worldwide, and 26 species native to North America. Fifty species of *Senna* are used in agriculture. *Senna* is widely distributed throughout North America, with the greatest diversity of species in the southern half of North America. Habitat varies by species, but most are found in moist, open woods and disturbed habitats.

TOXIC AGENT(S): The seeds of *Senna* contain sennosides that are commonly used to treat constipation. At therapeutic doses, treatment is generally believed to be safe and effective. Recent research suggests that the potential for toxicity of some *Senna* species has been greatly underestimated, possibly due to the presence of certain anthraquinones. The published literature includes multiple cases of fatal poisoning or serious liver damage caused by consumption of products containing *Senna*. In one case, a previously healthy woman who used *Senna* products for multiple weeks developed nausea, vomiting, and diarrhea. Blood tests revealed she was suffering from acute liver failure, and she died several days later, despite medical intervention. Another case involves hundreds of children who developed acute hepatomyoencephalopathy (HME) syndrome after consuming *Senna occidentalis*. HME is a multisystem failure of the liver, muscles, and brain with a 75% fatality rate. Over 500 children from this region died of HME each year until the culprit was finally identified in 2007. Despite these documented cases (and others), there is not complete agreement on the toxicity of *Senna*.

SIGNS AND SYMPTOMS OF POISONING: Exposure to toxins is through consumption of *Senna* seeds or use of plant extracts for tea or medicine. Poisoning may be chronic or acute. Chronic poisoning typically resolves with removal of the toxin. Clinical signs of acute poisoning include vomiting and diarrhea, followed by HME syndrome and death within 48 hours.

Sesbania vesicaria

BAG POD, BLADDERPOD, RATTLEBOX, OTHERS

Sesbania from the Arabic vernacular name for this plant (saisaban), *vesicaria* from the Latin word for bladder.

Fabaceae (Legume Family)

DESCRIPTION: *Sesbania vesicaria* is a tall (up to 2.5 m) legume with pinnately compound leaves—this means the leaf is organized into smaller parts called leaflets that are arranged across from each other on a stem-like structure called a rachis. Flowers have a standard "pea plant" floral morphology composed of a banner, wings, and keel. Seeds are contained in bean pods with pointed ends. The plant is referred to by several common names that reference the large bean seeds loosely contained in pods, causing them to rattle.

DISTRIBUTION AND HABITAT: *Sesbania vesicaria* is native to the southern United States and northern Mexico. It is more frequently found in wet meadows and other wetlands in the coastal plains. It cannot survive in a saline environment. It is often found as a weed growing in newly disturbed areas.

TOXIC AGENT(S): The toxicity of *Sesbania vesicaria* is intriguing. In many published sources, *S. vesicaria* is one of the most toxic of the *Sesbania* species. This claim is supported by numerous reports of sudden animal death, particularly after consuming dried plants. A toxin called sesbanimide was isolated from fresh beans of several *Sesbania* species, including *S. vesicaria.* It was later determined that this presumably plant-derived toxin has a structure nearly identical to cycloheximide, an antifungal produced by a bacterium. Upon further evaluation, it was concluded that although present in the beans, sesbanimide is produced by a bacterium and not the plant. Additional research has identified three saponins in the plant tissue that are likely toxic, but it is still unclear how these toxins may be interacting to create a deadly cocktail. It is believed that the toxin(s) accumulate in the body with repeated exposures. In certain conditions, animals and people can consume *S. vesicaria* with no known ill effects, and under a different set of conditions, consumption may be deadly.

SIGNS AND SYMPTOMS OF POISONING: Exposure to toxins is always through ingestion of plant material. Consumption of 0.1% body weight in seeds over multiple days is reported as a potentially fatal dose. Sesbanimide toxin functions in part by inhibiting protein synthesis and damaging DNA. Exposure to even a small quantity can cause tremors, seizures, coma, and death. There are quite likely multiple toxins involved in *Sesbania* intoxication, with specific saponins suspected to work in tandem with sesbanimide. Poisoning may occur over multiple days.

Solanum carolinense

HORSE NETTLE, APPLE OF SODOM, DEVIL'S TOMATO

Solanum from either the Latin word for "of the sun" (solanus) or the Latin word for soothing (solornus), *carolinense* for Carolinas.

Solanaceae (Nightshade Family)

DESCRIPTION: *Solanum carolinense* is a perennial herb, reaching about 1 m tall. The stem is covered with short, sharp spines, making it painful to remove the plant by hand. Large, triangular leaves with shallow lobes are arranged along the stem in an alternating pattern. Flowers have five petals, fused at the base, with prominent yellow anthers. The fruits are berries. Before ripening, they typically have light green or white striping along the top, and at maturity, they are an appealing, glossy yellow.

DISTRIBUTION AND HABITAT: *Solanum carolinense* is native to the southeastern coastal United States, but has spread throughout North America, except parts of the northwest. It is considered a noxious weed in many areas and can frequently be found in cropland and other disturbed areas.

TOXIC AGENT(S): All parts of the plant are toxic, and concentrations of solanine can vary greatly under different growing conditions. Fruits and seeds are the most toxic—with green, immature berries believed to be responsible for most cases of poisoning. The primary toxic agent in *Solanum carolinense* is the glycoalkaloid solanine. The precise mode of action is not fully understood, but it is believed to disrupt cell membranes, triggering cell damage and cell death. There is also speculation that solanine can cause congenital disabilities.

SIGNS AND SYMPTOMS OF POISONING: Exposure to toxins is through ingestion of plant material, primarily berries. Solanine poisoning in humans due to consumption of *Solanum* species is somewhat common, with several thousand cases, including dozens of deaths, reported in the literature. Hay and silage made from *Solanum carolinense* is reported to be responsible for livestock poisonings and death. In milder cases, symptoms are like food poisoning, including weakness, diarrhea, vomiting, and headache. In more serious cases, fever, respiratory distress, and death may occur.

Sorghum spp.

JOHNSON GRASS, SORGHUM

Sorghum from the Italian word for sorghum (sorgo).

Poaceae (Grass Family)

DESCRIPTION: *Sorghum* species superficially resemble corn but have inflorescences in the form of a panicle and flower spikelets borne in pairs. Side shoots are often produced, which lead to multiple flower heads on one plant. *Sorghum* produces a root system that is much more extensively branched than corn. Leaves usually have a waxy coating.

DISTRIBUTION AND HABITAT: There are 25 species of *Sorghum*, some of which are grown as a food crop, or as livestock forage. Most species are found in tropical and subtropical areas of the Eastern Hemisphere, with one species native to Mexico. Two species have been introduced to North America and are widely distributed throughout, with about 5 million acres planted each growing season.

TOXIC AGENT(S): The toxins of concern are cyanide and nitrate. All parts of the plant can be very toxic under certain conditions. *Sorghum* is a cyanogenetic plant, meaning it produces cyanogenic glycosides that can break down into hydrogen cyanide (sometimes called prussic acid) when exposed to certain plant enzymes. Early growing season *Sorghum* that has been damaged by frost may have very high levels of prussic acid, and silage may contain high levels of toxic HCN gas. Cyanide prevents oxygen from releasing from hemoglobin, causing cellular hypoxia and anoxia.

SIGNS AND SYMPTOMS OF POISONING: Exposure to toxins is primarily through ingestion of plant material. Symptoms of cyanide poisoning tend to occur very rapidly, following ingestion. Initial symptoms may include tremors, spasms, and vomiting, followed by labored breathing, seizures, loss of consciousness, cardiac arrest, and possibly death.

Stillingia spp.

QUEEN'S DELIGHT, TOOTHLEAF

Stillingia for Benjamin Stillingfleet, British botanist.

Euphorbiaceae (Spurge Family)

DESCRIPTION: *Stillingia* spp. are annual or perennial herbaceous plants or subshrubs, ranging from 25 cm to 1 m in height. Stems and leaves contain a toxic, milky sap. Leaves in most species are alternate, and can be linear, lanceolate, or obovate, with either entire or dentate margins and a shiny green color. Leaves have tiny, glandular teeth along the margins, which are referenced in one of its common names, Toothleaf. *Stillingia* is monoecious, meaning that individual male and female flowers are present on the same plant. Inconspicuous flowers are usually on spikes at the end of branches. Flowers are small and greenish yellow. Fruits are capsules.

DISTRIBUTION AND HABITAT: *Stillingia* is a genus of 33 species, seven of which are found in North America. *Stillingia* can be found throughout the southern United States, Mexico, and Central America. They tend to be found in open, dry, sandy habitats, although some species are found in wetland habitats.

TOXIC AGENT(S): All parts of the plant are toxic, but the roots are believed to contain the highest concentrations of toxins. *Stillingia* is reported to have cyanogenic glycosides—compounds that are converted to cyanide during the process of digestion. Other compounds in the plant are said to be skin and mucous membrane irritants, although not considered to be toxic. Dangerous concentrations are found in dried or cut leaves. Cyanide prevents the release of oxygen from hemoglobin, leading to anoxia. Toxic levels of some heavy metals have also been reported, which may be a contributing toxicity factor.

SIGNS AND SYMPTOMS OF POISONING: Exposure to toxins is through ingestion of dry or fresh plant materials, but most fatal poisonings in livestock occur while grazing on dried plant material. Ruminant animals appear to be most susceptible to poisoning, likely due to bacteria in the ruminate digestion. Cyanide is fast acting, and signs of poisoning will occur within minutes of reaching the lethal dose. These include tremors, weakness, dizziness, vertigo, and difficulty breathing, progressing to coma and death within 15 minutes to several hours.

Symphytum officinale

COMFREY

**Symphytum from the Ancient Greek word for comfrey (súmphuton),
officinale from the Italian word for medicinal (officinale).**

Boraginaceae (Borage Family)

DESCRIPTION: *Symphytum officinale* is a perennial flowering plant growing about 100 cm tall and 50 cm wide, with attractive, bright green foliage. The entire plant is lightly covered with stiff hairs. The leaves are large (10–20 cm long and 2–10 cm wide) and ovate. Leaves are alternate at the bottom of the stem and opposite toward the top of the stem. Flowers are dark purple, bell-shaped, and clustered on a scorpiod cyme (curved, like a scorpion tail) inflorescence. It also has a characteristic dark, thick taproot.

DISTRIBUTION AND HABITAT: *Symphytum officinale* is native to Europe and parts of Asia. It was brought to North American by European settlers for use as a medicinal herb. It is still a common garden plant, and it has escaped cultivation to become broadly distributed in North America, except the Great Plains and Mexico. It can be found in shady, disturbed areas such as vacant lots, along roadsides, and in ditches.

TOXIC AGENT(S): Despite being used as a medicinal herb for several thousand years, dietary supplements and teas containing comfrey were banned by regulatory agencies in the United States, Canada, and many European countries when it was discovered they may cause liver failure and cancer. The toxic agents responsible include the pyrrolizidine alkaloids lasiocarpine and symphytine. When these alkaloids are metabolized in the liver, they are converted to highly reactive pyrroles that cause cellular dysfunction, disrupt cell division, and kill cells. There are multiple reported cases of large-scale human fatalities due to acute poisoning by pyrrolizidine alkaloids. The largest occurred in the Gulran District of western Afghanistan between 1974 and 1976, when nearly 8,000 people consumed bread made with wheat contaminated with seeds from a local weed known to produce pyrrolizidine alkaloids. At least 1,600 people died in that case, with likely many more deaths unreported.

SIGNS AND SYMPTOMS OF POISONING: Exposure to toxins is through ingestion. Poisoning can be chronic or acute. Chronic cases involve repeated low-dose exposures of toxins, often from dietary supplements or tea. This may occur over multiple weeks. In these cases, liver tissues are repeatedly injured and healed, and the microscopic veins of the liver become clogged or destroyed, preventing blood flow into and out of the small blood vessels in the liver. In the early stages of chronic poisoning, there may be no symptoms. Once liver function is sufficiently compromised, clinical signs will include fluid buildup in the abdomen (ascites), jaundice, cirrhosis, and liver failure. Acute cases may present with more immediate signs, including a rapid onset of massive ascites and more severe liver damage.

Taxus spp.

YEW

Taxus from the Latin word for Yew.

Taxaceae (Yew Family)

DESCRIPTION: *Taxus* spp. are coniferous shrubs or small trees (usually up to 15 m). Landscape specimens are often pruned to rounded or squared shrubs. The bark is reddish brown in color, with a scaly appearance. Needles, which often appear two-ranked (meaning that the leaves are in two vertical columns on opposite sides of the stem), are soft, flat, and green, with a pointed tip that is not sharp to the touch. Needles have two pale green strips on the lower surface. Single seeds are contained within a red, fleshy, cuplike structure called an aril.

DISTRIBUTION AND HABITAT: *Taxus* is a genus of six to ten species, with three species native to North America, along with a handful of cultivated varieties used extensively as landscape plants. Native and cultivated species are widespread throughout North America. Habitat includes mixed-conifer hardwood forests, swamps, and ravines.

TOXIC AGENT(S): All parts of the Yew, except the aril, contain taxine alkaloids. Taxines are cardiotoxins that interfere with the function of cells responsible for contracting the heart muscle. Upon ingestion, they are quickly absorbed in the intestine, resulting in cardiac arrest or respiratory failure if a fatal dose is consumed. A dose of 3 mg/kg is thought to be the lethal dose in humans, and the prognosis is grim even with medical intervention. Although taxines have a mode of action and clinical signs similar to digoxin, the digoxin antidote is usually not effective.

SIGNS AND SYMPTOMS OF POISONING: Exposure to toxins is primarily through ingestion of needles, bark, and seeds. Accidental poisoning is not uncommon in children under three, due to the attractive red arils frequently found on the common landscape trees. Signs of poisoning include nausea, vomiting, diarrhea, headache, dizziness, tremors, shortness of breath, irregular or slowed heart rate, and death by heart failure.

Triglochin maritima

ARROWGRASS, POD GRASS, GOOSEGRASS

Triglochin **from the Latin word for three (tri) and the Greek word for points (glochin),** *maritima* **from the Latin word for "of the sea."**

Juncaginaceae (Arrowgrass Family)

DESCRIPTION: *Triglochin maritima* are herbaceous perennials reaching up to 60 cm in height. Leaves are basal and grasslike, and up to 20 cm long. Flowers are borne on dense spikes that are taller than the leaves. Individual flowers are very small and lack petals, with just the male and female structures present. Fruits are cylindrical and divided into three narrow sections.

DISTRIBUTION AND HABITAT: *Triglochin maritima* is found throughout temperate parts of the Northern Hemisphere. In North America, it can be found in suitable habitats throughout most of the West, the Midwest, and northeastern North America. It is a species found in marshy areas along the coast and at high elevations, as well as alkaline wetlands in inland areas.

TOXIC AGENT(S): *Triglochin maritima* contains a cyanogenic glycoside called triglochinin, which can be found in all parts of the plant. It is thought that the plant only produces triglochinin in new growth or when it is stressed, such as during drought conditions. During digestion, triglochinin gets converted into cyanide, which prevents the release of oxygen from hemoglobin, leading to anoxia. Even in small amounts, it is highly toxic to ruminants, due to the nature of their digestive systems. Very large quantities would need to be consumed by a human to cause death.

SIGNS AND SYMPTOMS OF POISONING: Exposure to toxins is through ingestion of dry or fresh plant materials, but most fatal poisonings in livestock occur while grazing on dried plant material. Ruminant animals appear to be most susceptible to poisoning, likely due to bacteria in the ruminate digestion. Cyanide is fast acting, and signs of poisoning occur within minutes of reaching the lethal dose. These include tremors, weakness, dizziness, vertigo, and difficulty breathing, progressing to coma and death within 15 minutes to several hours.

Veratrum spp.

FALSE HELLEBORE, CORN LILY

Veratrum from the Latin words for true (vere) and black (ater).

Melanthiacaeae (Bunchflower Family)

DESCRIPTION: *Veratrum* spp. are perennials that grow from a basal bulb, with hollow, leafy stems. The alternate leaves are generally broadly rounded in shape and are usually keeled, or partially folded around the stem. Leaves get smaller and more crowded as you go up the stem, overlapping each other. Flowers are borne on terminal racemes or panicles. Individual flowers bear six tepals that can be white, green, yellow, or purple in color.

DISTRIBUTION AND HABITAT: *Veratrum* is a group of about 30 species, five of which can be found in temperate regions of North America. Preferential habitat includes sunny, open areas with deep, moist soils, such as wet meadows and swamps.

TOXIC AGENT(S): Toxic components can be found in all parts of the plant but are most concentrated in the roots. Several alkaloids are produced, but veratridine is the most clinically significant. It is a neurotoxin that increases activation of cardiac and skeletal muscles. Toxins are only produced during periods of active growth and are deactivated when the plant is dormant. A nontoxic compound is also present, 2-deoxyjervine, which can cause cyclopism in developing embryos.

SIGNS AND SYMPTOMS OF POISONING: Exposure to toxins is through ingestion of plant material. Clinical signs include severe nausea, bradycardia, hypotension, salivation, weakness, difficulty breathing, and possibly death.

Xanthium strumarium

COCKLEBUR

Xanthium from the Greek word for yellow (xanthos),
strumarium from the Greek word for swelling.
Both refer to the appearance of the seeds as they develop.

Asteraceae (Aster Family)

DESCRIPTION: *Xanthium strumarium* is an annual herbaceous weed that grows to 2 m tall. It has broad, triangular leaves that alternate on a stout stem. The entire plant is covered with bristly hairs. Flowers are small and inconspicuous and produce a characteristic fruit covered with spiny hooks known as a "Cocklebur" or bur. Each Cocklebur contains two seeds: a large, nondormant seed that can germinate immediately, and a smaller, dormant seed that will germinate later, after the right conditions have been met.

DISTRIBUTION AND HABITAT: *Xanthium strumarium* is distributed throughout North America. It is primarily found in disturbed open areas and is a common, destructive weed in agricultural settings.

TOXIC AGENT(S): *Xanthium strumarium* produces the toxic diterpene glycoside carboxyatractyloside. All plant parts should be considered toxic, but toxins are most highly concentrated in the seeds. It functions by inhibiting oxidative phosphorylation—the final step of a cellular biochemical process to transform food into a form of cellular energy called ATP. It is theorized that a primary function of carboxyatractyloside in *X. strumarium* is to repress the development of one seed, keeping it in a dormant state. Carboxyatractyloside is highly toxic to humans and animals.

SIGNS AND SYMPTOMS OF POISONING: Exposure in humans is primarily due to accidental ingestion of seeds or ingestion in cases of extreme food scarcity. In reported cases, consumption of 40 or more seeds resulted in a mortality rate of about 25%. In one case study, 76 individuals ate *X. strumarium* seeds prepared as a main meal; 19 died, despite medical intervention. Other reported cases included fatalities and multiorgan failures, one case necessitating a liver transplant. Signs of intoxication begin approximately 12–24 hours after ingestion. Individuals seeking treatment experienced acute gastrointestinal disturbances, nausea, profuse sweating, weakness, and convulsions. Poisoning may cause multiorgan failure, and death may occur as soon as 48 hours after ingestion.

Zamia integrifolia

ZAMIA, COONTIE PALM, FLORIDA ARROWROOT

**Zamia from the Latin word for pinecone,
integrifolia from the Latin word for undivided leaves.**

Zamiaceae (Zamia Family)

DESCRIPTION: *Zamia integrifolia* is a low-growing species of Cycad, with large (up to 100 cm) compound leaves containing 5–30 pairs of leaflets. Leaflets are linear and narrow in shape, very stiff, and colored a dark, glossy green. Leaflets are often twisted, and can be either toothless or have small teeth near the tip. Leaflet edges are often revolute. *Zamia integrifolia* is dioecious, so plants are either male or female, with cylindrical cones that can reach up to 20 cm in length.

DISTRIBUTION AND HABITAT: *Zamia integrifolia* is native to the southeastern United States and the West Indies. It is usually observed growing in scrubby pine or oak woodlands. Populations are in decline, and it is considered an endangered species in Florida.

TOXIC AGENT(S): The entire plant is toxic. The toxic glycoside cycasin is found in all plant tissues. The seeds contain an additional toxic glycoside and an amino acid called β-methylamino l-alanine (BMAA). Cycasin is acted upon by enzymes found in the stomachs of mammals that cause the formation of methylazoxymethanol (MAM), which then breaks down into formaldehyde and diazomethane. This causes irritation of the GI tract and liver cell necrosis. In addition, diazomethane also methylates DNA, which is potentially carcinogenic. Despite the severity of these toxins, they are water soluble, and indigenous people of the region developed methods to extract the toxins and create an edible starch from ground root tissues. European settlers learned from the indigenous tribes, and most people had backyard mills for processing *Zamia* roots as a cash crop, referred to as Florida Arrowroot. The commercial industry grew, and during WWI, gruel made from the starch was the first nourishment gassed soldiers could keep down. The last commercial mill stopped production in 1926 as *Zamia* became increasingly scarce.

SIGNS AND SYMPTOMS OF POISONING: Exposure to toxins is through ingestion of plant material, or improperly prepared starch products. Signs of poisoning typically occur within 12 hours of ingestions. Signs include severe gastrointestinal symptoms (diarrhea, vomiting, etc.), weakness, lethargy, seizures, and coma. Death due to liver failure usually occurs only when there is no medical intervention.

Zigadenus spp.

DEATHCAMAS, DEATH CAMAS, NUTTALL'S DEATH CAMAS, POISON ONION

Zigadenus from the Greek words for yoke (zugon) and gland
(adenas), which refer to the pair of glands present
at the base of the flower's tepals.

Liliaceae (Lily Family)

DESCRIPTION: *Zigadenus* is an early spring flowering plant that first produces long, grasslike leaves, followed by a long (20 cm) flower stalk. Approximately 20–50 flowers are arranged on the stem in a cylindrical cluster or raceme. Flowers are typically white or light pink, with six petals. Plants die back by early summer, leaving a large, dark,underground bulb that somewhat resembles a wild onion but lacks the distinctive onion odor.

DISTRIBUTION AND HABITAT: There are at least 18 *Zigadenus* species native to North America; however, the taxonomy for this genus is still under revision. It is distributed throughout the southwestern and southeastern United States, with the greatest species diversity in the southwest. It is found in many different, species-specific habitats.

TOXIC AGENT(S): All plant parts should be considered toxic, but the highest concentrations of steroidal alkaloids have been isolated from bulbs and dried plant materials. Several steroidal alkaloids have been isolated from *Zigadenus*, including germine, pertoverine, and zygacine. The precise mode of action is not fully understood for these toxins, but it is in part due to their ability to alter sodium ion transport in cells and thereby disrupt essential cellular functions.

SIGNS AND SYMPTOMS OF POISONING: Exposure to toxins is through ingestion of plant material. This plant may poison all humans and animals, but sheep seem to be the most susceptible, with reports of up to 500 sheep killed in one incident. Human poisoning occurs when the *Z. nuttallii* bulb is confused with wild onion or other edible bulbs. Poisoning is dose dependent; mild poisoning may manifest as burning mouth and lips, vomiting, and frothy salivation. High doses may cause a dangerously low and irregular heartbeat, difficulty breathing, and death.

Amanita bisporigera

DESTROYING ANGEL

**Amanita from the Ancient Greek word
for mushroom (amanites), *bisporigera* is of mixed origin,
but roughly translates to "having two spores."**

Amanitaceae

DESCRIPTION: The name "Destroying Angel" is commonly applied to several *Amanita* species that are nearly or completely all white. Visual identification of *Amanita bisporigera* is not reliable, due to many look-alike species, with chemical and microscopic examination required to identify the species. The true *A. bisporigera* is a predominantly all-white (stem, cap, and gills) mushroom, ranging from 5 cm to 15 cm in height, with a cap 2.5–10 cm in width. The cap may change to a pale tan or pale pink color when old, or during particularly hot and dry weather. Partial veil remnants are sometimes present as a slight flocculence (wooly tufts) around the cap margin, especially in young caps. The cap color will change to yellow where more than 5% potassium hydroxide is applied. Near the top of the stem, under the cap, hangs a thin, delicate, skirt-like ring that occasionally becomes shredded or slips down the stem. The base of the stem, typically buried underground, is swollen and covered by a volva (sack-like structure) that extends up to 4 cm from the base of the stem. Stem and cap flesh are white and don't change color when cut and exposed to air. The odor has been described as faintly pleasant in young specimens, but turns sickeningly sweet with age. The Meixner-Wieland test is a simple test that can help determine the species: juice from the mushroom is rubbed onto a newspaper, then hydrochloric acid is applied to the newspaper. The color will turn blue if amatoxins are present.

DISTRIBUTION AND HABITAT: *Amanita bisporigera* is only known to be found in the eastern Americas, from Newfoundland to Texas. It is primarily found in forest habitats containing pine or oak species. There is some evidence that it has possibly been unintentionally introduced to pine plantations in Columbia.

TOXIC AGENT(S): *Amanita bisporigera* is considered deadly poisonous and is perhaps the deadliest mushroom in North America. It should become very familiar, along with its look-alikes, to those collecting mushrooms for consumption in eastern North America. The principal toxic component is an amatoxin called amanitin. The toxin inhibits the RNA polymerase II enzyme, which is involved in DNA transcription, RNA production, and protein synthesis. The lethal dose of amanitin is 0.1 mg/kg of body weight. For example, the lethal dose for a 68-kg person is 6.8 mg. One mature mushroom contains 10–12 mg of amanitin.

SIGNS AND SYMPTOMS OF POISONING: Exposure to toxins is through ingestion. After ingestion and uptake, amanitin effectively causes liver cells to burst (cytolysis). Symptoms usually don't manifest themselves until 10–24 hours after ingestion, which is one reason this toxin is so deadly. The first symptoms to appear are usually diarrhea and cramps, but they often fade away, giving a false sense of relief. By the fifth day after ingestion, the toxin starts having significant effects on the liver and kidneys, leading to their complete failure, which leads to coma, respiratory failure, and then death. Around 15% of people will die by the tenth day after ingestion. Those that survive usually are left with permanent liver damage.

Amanita pantherina sensu lato

PANTHER CAP, MANY OTHERS

Amanita from the Ancient Greek word for mushroom (amanites),
pantherina from the Latin word for panther-like.

Amanitaceae

DESCRIPTION: What has traditionally been called *Amanita pantherina* in North America is actually several species that resemble *A. pantherina*, of which only some have been formally described (*A. ameripanthera, A. multisquamosa,* and *A. velatipes* are some of them). The true *Amanita pantherina* is native to Europe and western Asia. The North American species can reach 18 cm tall, and feature yellowish to dark brown caps that often are covered to some extent by white warts. The annulus (stem ring) is typically connected around the midpoint of the stem, and often will look funnel shaped. The top edge of the volva at the base of the stem is usually rolled in, giving the appearance of a collar.

DISTRIBUTION AND HABITAT: The North American Panther Cap species are broadly distributed throughout North America, usually in association with conifers or oak species. *A. ameripanthera* is associated with conifers in western North America, from British Columbia to California. *A. multisquamosa* and *A. velatipes* are eastern North American species associated with pine or oak forests.

TOXIC AGENT(S): The toxic agent and toxicity of the North American Panther Caps have not been fully resolved for all species, so consumption of any mushroom fitting the general description should be avoided. *A. pantherina* contains the toxin muscimol, and it is presumed that most, if not all, of the North American counterparts also contain muscimol. Muscimol is a potent $GABA_A$ receptor agonist, which results in an alteration of neuron activity in many areas of the brain.

SIGNS AND SYMPTOMS OF POISONING: Exposure to toxins is through ingestion. The effects of muscimol can begin as soon as 30 minutes after ingestion, although it can sometimes take up to a few hours. Initial symptoms can include feelings of euphoria, lucidity, and synesthesia. Less tolerable effects include nausea, excessive salivation, and muscle twitching. Large doses can result in delirium, hallucinations, and dissociation. Deaths caused by muscimol are very rare, but can happen, especially in children, the elderly, and those with underlying morbidities.

Amanita phalloides

DEATH CAP

Amanita from the Ancient Greek word for mushroom (amanites),
phalloides from the Ancient Greek word for phallic.

Amanitaceae

DESCRIPTION: Death Caps typically reach about 15 cm in height, with a cap that is equally as wide. Occasional specimens can reach nearly double this size, however. The stems can range from white to pale yellow, sometimes with darker yellow coloration near the base. A membranous ring is usually present in the upper portion of the stem, also ranging in color from white to pale yellow. The color of the cap is variable, often giving the impression of blotchy, multicolored fibers arranged concentrically. Shades of olive, greenish yellow, yellow, gray, and brown are typically seen. The colors are usually palest at the edge of the cap, with darker colors in the center, although it is not uncommon for the center to have a bleached appearance. Older specimens have been reported to have a sickeningly sweet odor that can be detected from a distance.

DISTRIBUTION AND HABITAT: The Death Cap is native to Europe, although it has been introduced to many countries around the world due to the exportation of trees with which it has a symbiotic relationship. In North America, it has been found from British Columbia south to California, as well as New England south to Virginia.

TOXIC AGENT(S): Death Caps contain the toxin amanitin, which was previously described under *Amanita bisporigera*, and are considered deadly poisonous. Most mushroom deaths worldwide are caused by Death Caps, with an average of one person per year dying in North America. Consumption of as little as half of a cap is thought to be enough to cause death in an adult human. Additionally, Death Caps contain several compounds called phallotoxins, which have been found to have red blood cell–destroying properties and are highly toxic to liver cells. Research has shown that phallotoxins do not add to the overall toxicity of the mushroom.

SIGNS AND SYMPTOMS OF POISONING: Exposure to toxins is through ingestion. After ingestion and uptake, amanitin effectively causes liver cells to burst (cytolysis). Symptoms usually don't manifest themselves until 10–24 hours after ingestion, which is one reason this toxin is so deadly. The first symptoms to appear are usually diarrhea and cramps, but they often fade away, giving a false sense of relief. By the fifth day after ingestion, the toxin starts having significant effects on the liver and kidneys, leading to their complete failure, which leads to coma, respiratory failure, and then death. Around 15% of people will die by the tenth day after ingestion. Those that survive usually are left with permanent liver damage.

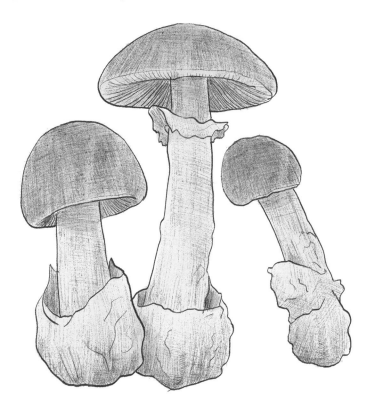

Aspergillus flavus

ASPERGILLUS

Aspergillus from the Latin word for a holy water sprinkler (aspergillium), flavus from the Latin word for yellow.

Trichocomaceae

DESCRIPTION: *Aspergillus flavus* is a common, soil-dwelling fungus that can become a pathogen of grains, beans, and nuts, as well as animals, including humans. Unlike most fungal pathogens, *A. flavus* prefers warm, dry conditions. Under these conditions, it can infect almost any crop seed, usually going unnoticed until after the seeds have been dried and stored. For example, during drought conditions, *A. flavus* is a common pathogen of corn, causing ear rot. While positive identification of *A. flavus* is only possible through microscopic analysis, infected plants or seeds usually will show some rot symptoms, such as discolored and broken-down tissue. When reaching the fruiting stage, the fungus will have a powdery appearance, and will be greenish yellow in color. In humans and other animals, it is an opportunistic pathogen, primarily in immunocompromised individuals. It is one of the leading causes of a disease called aspergillosis, which is the collective name for a wide range of symptoms caused by infections of several *Aspergillus* species.

DISTRIBUTION AND HABITAT: *A. flavus* has a worldwide distribution and is a common component of soil microflora, acting as a decomposer of organic matter. It is also likely to be present, to some degree, in most plant-based foods around the world.

TOXIC AGENT(S): Under the right conditions, which usually involve elevated moisture levels and a lack of competing organisms, *A. flavus* can produce several compounds that are collectively called aflatoxins. Ingestion of aflatoxins leads to both acute and chronic disease in humans. Susceptibility to aflatoxins varies widely between individuals, with sex, age, health, and fungal strain all being influential factors. Children are most susceptible to the effects of aflatoxins.

SIGNS AND SYMPTOMS OF POISONING: Exposure to toxins is through ingestion. Acute toxicity, resulting from large doses, destroys liver cells and causes acute liver failure. Symptoms include bleeding, edema, lethargy, and coma. When fatal, death is usually a result of liver cirrhosis. Chronic effects from exposure to small doses over an extended period have immunological and nutritional consequences. Aflatoxins can suppress the activity of several components of the immune system, leading to an increase in disease prevalence and severity. Aflatoxins also decrease the efficiency of the digestive system and can cause malnutrition and stunted growth. Both acute and chronic exposures increase the risk of developing cancers, especially liver cancer. Aflatoxins are one of the most potent naturally produced carcinogens known. The carcinogenicity is due to a by-product of the body's metabolism of aflatoxin, which results in the formation of a compound called an epoxide. Epoxides can readily bind to DNA, causing mutations that increase the risk of tumor formation.

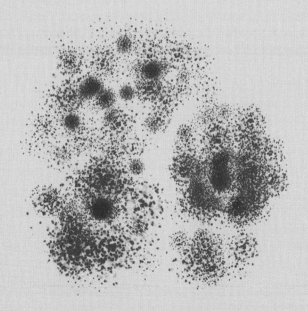

Chlorophyllum molybdites

FALSE PARASOL, GREEN-SPORED PARASOL, THE VOMITER

Chlorophyllum from the Ancient Greek words for green (khloros) and leaf (phullon), **molybdites** likely refers to the element molybdemum, or the mineral molybdite, and is derived from the Latin word for molybdenum (molybdaenum).

Agaricaceae

DESCRIPTION: The False Parasol is a striking mushroom, capable of reaching nearly a foot (30 cm) tall, with a cap equally as wide. The stem is typically white to brownish in color, often having a fibrous appearance, and adorned with a whitish ring in the upper portion. The cap color is whitish to pale tan, and it is covered with coarse, brownish scales concentrated near the center of the cap. Young caps are spherical but become nearly flat at maturity. The gill color starts out white but turns greenish with age, due to the greenish color of its spores.

DISTRIBUTION AND HABITAT: These mushrooms are mainly found in lawns and meadows, either solitary or often in scattered patches or "fairy rings." They are widely distributed across North America but are more commonly seen in eastern North America.

TOXIC AGENT(S): *Chlorophyllum molybdites* is probably the most common cause of mushroom poisoning in North America, due to its similarity to other edible species, especially young specimens. Several potentially toxic compounds have been isolated from this species, but the exact cause of toxicity has yet to be fully understood. There is some anecdotal evidence that the toxicity is variable, or that some people may be more immune to the effects than others.

SIGNS AND SYMPTOMS OF POISONING: Exposure to toxins is through ingestion. Symptoms typically occur within a couple of hours after ingestion, and are gastrointestinal in nature. They are often severe, and include nausea, vomiting, and diarrhea. While there has not been a reported death due to consumption of this mushroom, the symptoms can get severe enough to be fatal.

Claviceps **spp.**

ERGOT

Claviceps **from the Latin word for club headed.**

Clavicipitaceae

DESCRIPTION: *Claviceps* is a group of at least 50 species of fungi that infect the floral structures of many grass species, including economically important species such as rye, sorghum, wheat, and barley. Initial infection produces a soft, white-colored tissue among the florets. Honeydew is produced from this tissue and can be seen dripping from the florets. This honeydew contains spores, which are dispersed by insects that feed on the honeydew. Later, the soft tissue hardens and darkens, forming a structure called a sclerotium. This stage is visible as thick, dark, finger-shaped structures within the normal, uninfected florets. The sclerotium eventually falls to the ground and forms fruiting bodies that resemble tiny mushrooms, when conditions are favorable. These fruiting bodies disperse spores when suitable host species are producing flowers.

DISTRIBUTION AND HABITAT: *Claviceps* spp. can be found worldwide, wherever its host species grow or are cultivated.

TOXIC AGENT(S): The principal toxic agents in *Claviceps* are collectively referred to as ergot alkaloids, with at least 70 different alkaloids having been identified among the various species of *Claviceps*. They are produced in the sclerotium, resulting in the ingestion of contaminated grains, which causes most cases of poisoning. Their primary mode of action revolves around the activation or inhibition of adrenaline, dopamine, and serotonin.

SIGNS AND SYMPTOMS OF POISONING: Exposure to toxins is through ingestion. Symptoms are wide-ranging and governed by a complex set of factors, including the species of *Claviceps* involved, the species of host plant and the soil it is growing in, geographic location, time of year, dosage, and the individual's state of health, among others. These all influence both the type and quantity of alkaloids that will be synthesized by the fungus. Symptoms manifest themselves in two ways that are not necessarily mutually exclusive. One set of symptoms is related to the contraction of smooth muscle cells in the body. This results in diminished blood flow and oxygen supply to the body's tissues. Symptoms of this include vomiting, diarrhea, and tingling or numbness in the extremities (the cause of Saint Anthony's fire, a burning pain in the extremities caused by reduced blood circulation due to ergot poisoning). This is usually accompanied by the development of gangrenous tissue in the hands and feet. The other set of symptoms involves hallucinations and convulsions, as many ergot alkaloids are chemically like LSD. In fact, LSD was originally synthesized using lysergic acid that was derived from an ergot alkaloid called ergotamine. At one time, it was theorized that the Salem witch trials were a result of an ergot outbreak, although that theory has been largely rejected by most experts.

Clitocybe rivulosa

FOOL'S FUNNEL, FALSE CHAMPIGNON

***Clitocybe* from the Ancient Greek words for hill (klitus) and head (kube), *rivulosa* from the Latin word for channel or stream (rivus).**

Tricholomataceae

DESCRIPTION: These are small, nondescript, predominantly white mushrooms that are usually no more than 5–10 cm tall. The cap usually becomes concave with age. With gills that run down the upper portion of the stem (decurrent), the mushroom is funnel shaped when viewed from the side. In older mushrooms, the cap often develops cracks or fissures in the upper surface. This species resembles several edible species.

DISTRIBUTION AND HABITAT: This species can be found in the eastern and western parts of North America, as well as in Europe. It typically is found in grassy habitats, such as lawns or meadows, and often forms "fairy rings."

TOXIC AGENT(S): An alkaloid called muscarine is the toxin present in this species, and usually at concentrations where one whole mushroom would contain a lethal dose. Muscarine is a mimic of the neurotransmitter acetylcholine, and acts as a stimulant of the parasympathetic nervous system (PNS). The PNS is responsible for returning the body to a relaxed state after a stressful situation, as well as controlling processes such as digestion, urination, and sexual arousal.

SIGNS AND SYMPTOMS OF POISONING: Exposure to toxins is through ingestion. Symptoms usually appear within a couple of hours following ingestion, and include excessive salivation, lacrimation (tears), vomiting, diarrhea, abdominal pain, pupil constriction, and a decreased heart rate. Eventually, the body will enter circulatory shock due to low blood pressure and a decreased heart rate. Death can occur in as little as eight hours without treatment.

Cortinarius rubellus

DEADLY WEBCAP

Cortinarius from the Latin word for veiled,
rubellus **from the Latin word for reddish.**

Cortinariaceae

DESCRIPTION: These mushrooms can grow up to 13 cm tall, with a cap that can grow up to 9 cm wide. The cap color is typically some shade of brown, paler at the edge, and it is covered with fibrous scales. The gills are a pale brownish color when young, but turn darker brown with age. The stem is usually the same color as the cap, or somewhat paler, and often has yellowish veil remnants on the lower portion. It has been described by some people as having the odor of radishes.

DISTRIBUTION AND HABITAT: In North America, this species has been found on the West Coast from Washington to California, and on the East Coast from New York to Newfoundland. It is also found across most of Europe. It is usually found in moist conifer forests.

TOXIC AGENT(S): This species contains the toxin orellanine, which is unique among known mushroom toxins because it only affects the kidneys. The specific mode of action has yet to be fully understood, but it is believed to interfere with certain types of chemical reactions in the kidneys, resulting in the formation of superoxides, which are toxic at high concentrations.

SIGNS AND SYMPTOMS OF POISONING: Exposure to toxins is through ingestion. Symptoms of orellanine poisoning can take anywhere from three days to three weeks to begin showing. Early symptoms include vomiting, diarrhea, loss of appetite, headaches, and chills. Eventually, kidney failure occurs. Dialysis or a kidney transplant is needed to avoid death.

Galerina marginata

FUNERAL BELL

Galerina from the Latin word for helmet shaped, *marginata* from the Latin word for having a border (marginatus).

Hymenogastraceae

DESCRIPTION: The Funeral Bell is a small, orangish brown mushroom, usually growing no more than 5 cm tall or wide. The cap can be either flat or bell-shaped, and is noticeably sticky when moist. The cap color begins yellowish orange, becoming a darker orange-brown with age, and often develops a splotchy, two-toned appearance. Gills are yellowish at first, becoming a rusty brown with age. The stem can be whitish to brownish, and often darkens from the base upward as it ages. The stem often will have a bracelet-like ring, but not always.

DISTRIBUTION AND HABITAT: This species is well distributed across North America, anywhere forested habitats occur, and can be found at any time of the year. It is a saprobe, growing on rotting tree trunks that have fallen to the ground. It is usually found in clusters, but occasionally only a single mushroom will be seen.

TOXIC AGENT(S): This species contains amatoxins, and should be considered deadly poisonous. Amatoxins are a group of peptides produced by several types of mushrooms. They inhibit protein synthesis, which leads to the death of the cells that are affected.

SIGNS AND SYMPTOMS OF POISONING: Exposure to toxins is through ingestion. Common symptoms include nausea, diarrhea, dizziness, and breathing difficulties. Liver and kidney damage are the end result, and can be fatal.

Gyromitra esculenta

BRAIN MUSHROOM, FALSE MOREL

**Gyromitra from the Ancient Greek words for round (guros)
and girdle or headband (mitra), *esculenta* from the
Latin word for edible (esculentus).**

Discinaceae

DESCRIPTION: This mushroom reaches up to 10 cm in height and 13 cm in width. The cap is pinkish to reddish brown in color, often becoming very dark with age, and it has a highly convoluted, asymmetrical shape; hence the common name "Brain Mushroom." The lower surface of the cap is usually hidden from view, but is whitish in color and mealy. The stem is paler than the cap, usually pale tan to pale reddish brown in color, and is circular in cross section, but can become folded into a figure-eight shape. These mushrooms only appear in the spring, and are often encountered by those searching for Morels.

DISTRIBUTION AND HABITAT: *Gyromitra. esculenta* is widely distributed across North America, from Alaska to Mexico. It is particularly abundant in montane forests of the Pacific coast and forested parts of New England and the Upper Great Lakes. It is found in sandy, forested areas, primarily coniferous forests, but it has also been found in deciduous forests.

TOXIC AGENT(S): This species contains gyromitrin, which is hydrolyzed by the body to form the toxic substance monomethylhydrazine. This toxin acts on the central nervous system and has been shown to be carcinogenic in small mammals. Gyromitrin is a volatile substance, meaning it readily evaporates. Therefore, it is possible to inhale gyromitrin from these mushrooms when storing, drying, or boiling them.

SIGNS AND SYMPTOMS OF POISONING: Exposure to toxins is through ingestion. Symptoms occur within 6–12 hours after ingestion and are gastrointestinal and neurological in nature. Initial symptoms include nausea, diarrhea, and vomiting, followed by dizziness, lethargy, vertigo, and tremors. Fever is also often present, a symptom not reported from other mushroom toxins. For most people, recovery occurs within two to six days. However, some people will then experience more severe symptoms after one to three days of feeling better. These symptoms are due to kidney and liver damage, and are accompanied by neurological symptoms such as delirium, tremors, and seizures. In cases of severe poisoning, these symptoms are followed by coma and heart failure. Death usually occurs about a week after ingestion in those cases.

Hebeloma crustuliniforme

POISON PIE, FAIRY CAKE

Hebeloma from the Ancient Greek word for youth or vigor (hebe),
while *loma* is of unknown origin, but likely means fringe or veil.
Crustuliniforme is of unknown origin, but likely is derived
from Latin words that mean bread-like.

Hymenogastraceae

DESCRIPTION: This mushroom reaches up to 13 cm in height, with caps up to 11 cm wide. The cap usually is flat or bell-shaped, and is slimy when young. The cap color ranges from whitish to pale tan, and is often noticeably darker toward the center. The gills are pale tan when young and turn browner with age. Young gills frequently have beads of liquid along their edges, which leave dark brown spot stains as the gills age. The stem is typically whitish to pale tan and may be finely hairy. This species is found in woodlands and along woodland edges, primarily growing in clusters of 2–5 mushrooms, but sometimes in arcs or "fairy rings." It has been reported to have a smell similar to radishes and a bitter taste.

DISTRIBUTION AND HABITAT: It is widely distributed throughout most of North America, as far south as northern Mexico, but is notably absent from arid regions, such as the Great Plains and the Desert Southwest.

TOXIC AGENT(S): The chemical(s) produced by this species which induces poisoning in humans has not yet been discovered.

SIGNS AND SYMPTOMS OF POISONING: Exposure to toxins is through ingestion. Symptoms usually occur within a few hours after ingestion, and are typical gastrointestinal symptoms, such as nausea, cramping, vomiting, and diarrhea.

Hypholoma fasciculare

SULFUR TUFT, CLUSTERED WOODLOVER

Hypholoma from the Ancient Greek word for web (huphe), while *loma* is of unknown origin, but likely means fringe or veil. *Fasciculare* from either the Latin word for striped (fascicularis) or the Latin word for "things carried in bundles" (fascicularia).

Strophariaceae

DESCRIPTION: This mushroom reaches up to 13 cm in height, with caps up to 8 cm wide. The cap usually is convex to nearly flat. The cap color begins reddish brown, but fades to a golden yellow in age, often darker at the center. Wispy veil remnants are often seen around the cap edge. The gills are yellow when young and turn more of an olive color as they age, and ultimately become spotted dark purple to black. Stems are typically 1 cm wide, and colored similar to the cap, and they often develop darker colors near the base. The stems are often curved.

DISTRIBUTION AND HABITAT: This species is widely distributed across North America, primarily in northern, coastal, or mountainous woodlands. It has also been reported from every continent except Antarctica. This is a saprobic species, mostly found growing in clusters on decaying logs and stumps of both coniferous and deciduous trees. It is mostly found during periods of colder weather in the spring and fall seasons.

TOXIC AGENT(S): A terpenoid called fasciculol has been identified as a toxic agent in this species. There may be others yet to be discovered. While the exact mode of action has yet to be determined, there is evidence that the bioactivity is similar to amatoxins.

SIGNS AND SYMPTOMS OF POISONING: Exposure to toxins is through ingestion. Symptoms usually occur within a few hours after ingestion, and include diarrhea, vomiting, nausea, proteinuria, double vision, and collapse. It appears this mushroom is rarely fatal, but there is at least one human death attributed to consumption of this species. It has a very bitter taste that likely thwarts any attempts to consume it.

Inocybe lacera

TORN FIBRECAP

Inocybe from the Ancient Greek words for muscle (is) and head (kube), *lacera* from the Latin word for lacerated.

Inocybaceae

DESCRIPTION: This is one of many mushroom species commonly referred to as LBMs, or little brown mushrooms, because that's what they are. This species reaches about 4 cm in height, with a cap 4 cm wide. The cap is broadly convex, often with an umbo (a nipple-like structure in the center of the cap), and brown in color. The cap surface is densely fibrous or scaly, and often cracks or has a torn appearance. Young gills have a pale color that becomes brown with age, often with a white edge. The stem is about 1 cm wide and has a pale brown color. It can be either smooth or finely hairy, and occasionally will have a thin ring.

DISTRIBUTION AND HABITAT: This species is broadly distributed throughout North America, as far south as northern Mexico. It is absent from the more arid regions of North America. This species associates with a wide variety of trees, and is typically found during the summer and fall, growing either as a solitary individual, in scattered patches, or in clusters.

TOXIC AGENT(S): An alkaloid called muscarine is the toxin present in this species. Muscarine is a mimic of the neurotransmitter acetylcholine, and acts as a stimulant of the parasympathetic nervous system (PNS). The PNS is responsible for returning the body to a relaxed state after a stressful situation, as well as controlling processes such as digestion, urination, and sexual arousal.

SIGNS AND SYMPTOMS OF POISONING: Exposure to toxins is through ingestion. Symptoms usually appear within a couple of hours following ingestion, and include excessive salivation, lacrimation (tears), vomiting, diarrhea, abdominal pain, pupil constriction, and a decreased heart rate. Eventually, the body will enter circulatory shock due to low blood pressure and a decreased heart rate. Death can occur in as little as eight hours without treatment.

Lepiota subincarnata

FATAL DAPPERLING

Lepiota from the Ancient Greek words for scale (lepis) and ear (ous), *subincarnata* from the Latin words for "almost red," or pink.

Agaricaceae

DESCRIPTION: *Lepiota subincarnata* is a small, common mushroom of lawns and forested habitats. It grows up to 6 cm tall on a thin (0.5 cm) stem, with a cap that is about 4 cm in width. The cap starts out with a convex shape, and flattens out with age. The cap is covered by a pinkish brown, grainy-looking layer that cracks apart as the cap flattens out, giving the cap a scaly appearance.

DISTRIBUTION AND HABITAT: It can be found along the West Coast from British Columbia to California, as well as in the eastern Great Lakes region. It is also found in parts of Europe and Asia. This is a saprobic species, growing from fallen leaves and other vegetative material that falls to the ground.

TOXIC AGENT(S): This species contains amatoxins, and should be considered deadly poisonous. Amatoxins are a group of peptides produced by several types of mushrooms. They inhibit protein synthesis, which leads to the death of the cells that are affected.

SIGNS AND SYMPTOMS OF POISONING: Exposure to toxins is through ingestion. Common symptoms include nausea, diarrhea, dizziness, and breathing difficulties. Liver and kidney damage are the end result, and can be fatal.

Letharia vulpina

WOLF LICHEN, WOLF MOSS

Letharia from the Latin word for lethal (letalis), *vulpina* from the Latin word for fox (vulpinus).

Parmeliaceae

DESCRIPTION: *Letharia vulpina* is a lichenized fungus that was historically used to poison wolves and foxes, as well as providing a source of dye for Native Americans. The lichen has the overall appearance of a tiny, densely branched shrub, up to 10 cm across. It ranges in color from golden yellow to chartreuse, and usually has a roughened or grainy surface texture due to reproductive structures.

DISTRIBUTION AND HABITAT: Wolf Lichens are found along the West Coast, from British Columbia to California, and in the northern Rocky Mountains. They grow from the bark of conifer trees.

TOXIC AGENT(S): Vulpinic acid, which is synthesized by the fungal partner of the lichen symbiosis, is responsible for the yellow coloration of the lichen. It is thought to act as an herbivore deterrent, as well as shielding the lichen from blue light. It is considered to be a cytotoxin (kills cells) that is moderately toxic to meat-eating mammals.

SIGNS AND SYMPTOMS OF POISONING: Exposure to toxins is through ingestion. Due to its toxicity to mammals, and its effects on human cells in laboratory experiments, vulpinic acid is believed to be toxic to humans. However, its actual effect on humans is largely unknown, because there have been no reported cases of humans consuming these lichens. Scientists are discovering that vulpinic acid may have some beneficial effects on humans at low doses, including antimicrobial and anticancer properties.

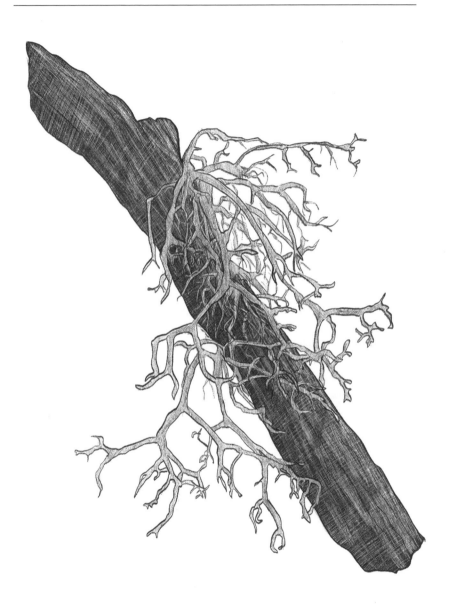

Omphalotus spp.

JACK-O'-LANTERN MUSHROOM, GHOST FUNGUS

Omphalotus from the Ancient Greek word for navel (omphalos).

Marasmiaceae

DESCRIPTION: The genus *Omphalotus* is composed of nine species, all of which are presumed to be poisonous. Some species are bioluminescent; hence the name "Jack-o'-Lantern Mushroom." The North American species are all large mushrooms that are almost always some shade of orange. One species from Mexico has a dark blue cap with white gills. These mushrooms can reach up to 15 cm tall, with caps up to 18 cm across, which are mostly concave, or funnel shaped. The gills are attached to the stem and partially run down it. The stem is thick (4 cm) and usually tough and fibrous. They superficially resemble the popular edible chanterelle mushrooms.

DISTRIBUTION AND HABITAT: *Omphalotus* species are widely distributed across eastern and western North America, and down through Mexico, while being mostly absent from the Great Plains. They are usually found growing in clusters from dead tree stumps or dead tree roots underground.

TOXIC AGENT(S): Two terpenes called Illudin S and Illudin M have been identified. They interact with DNA and disrupt the process of transcription. This ultimately impacts the synthesis of proteins in the body.

SIGNS AND SYMPTOMS OF POISONING: Exposure to toxins is through ingestion. Within a couple of hours of ingestion, stomach cramps, diarrhea, and vomiting present themselves and can last a couple of days. While there are no reported human deaths from Jack-o'-Lantern Mushroom poisoning, there have been documented cases of animal deaths, and it should be considered potentially lethal.

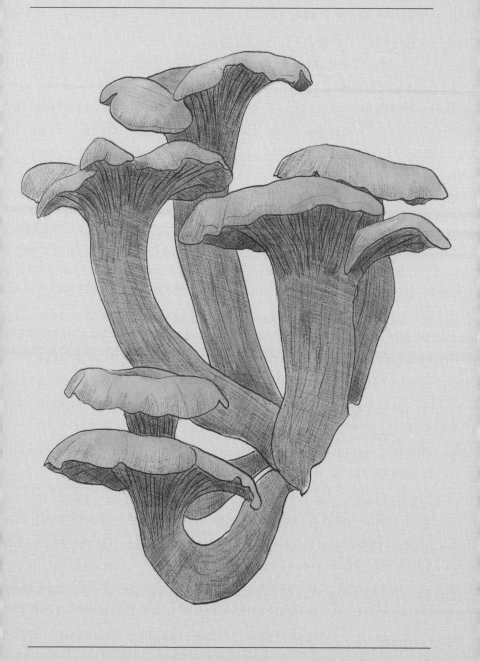

Paxillus involutus

BROWN ROLL-RIM, CINNAMON ROLL-RIM

Paxillus from the Latin word for peg (palus), *involutus* from the Latin word for rolled in (involvo).

Paxillaceae

DESCRIPTION: These mushrooms reach up to 8 cm in height, with caps reaching up to 15 cm across. The caps mostly have a broad, convex shape, although sometimes the central portion becomes depressed. The cap color can be somewhat variable, but is usually some shade of brown. The edge of the cap has a cottony appearance and is noticeably rolled in. The gills run down the stem and start out a pale ochre color, turning brown with age. Stems are typically up to 2 cm thick and tend to taper to the base. They are usually of a similar color to the cap, and will bruise brownish red when handled.

DISTRIBUTION AND HABITAT: This species is widely distributed throughout most of North America, tending to be absent in the more arid regions. It is also found throughout Europe and western Asia. It is mycorrhizal with a variety of tree species, and may be found growing solitary, or in scattered to dense clusters.

TOXIC AGENT(S): The toxic agent from these mushrooms has yet to be identified. However, it is known that it triggers an autoimmune reaction that causes the body's immune system to attack red blood cells. Therefore, the agent is technically not poisonous. It is believed that this autoimmune reaction develops after repeated consumption of the mushroom over a period of time, and the individual becomes hypersensitive to the agent.

SIGNS AND SYMPTOMS OF POISONING: Exposure to toxins is through ingestion. Initial symptoms are abdominal in nature (vomiting, diarrhea, etc.). Shortly thereafter, hemolysis and anemia develop, which leads to numerous health complications that can lead to death, even with medical intervention. Those that survive will still be left with serious health complications.

Pholiotina rugosa

CONECAP

**Pholiotina is of unknown origin, *rugosa* from the
Latin word for wrinkled (rugosus).**

Bolbitiaceae

DESCRIPTION: This is another LBM that superficially is indistinct from many other LBMs. This particular species reaches about 4 cm tall, with a cap up to 2 cm in diameter, and a thin (less than 3 mm) stem. Young caps are broadly cone shaped but become more rounded with age. The cap color is an orangish brown that fades to a paler shade around the periphery. Small lines, or striations, can be seen along the edge in this paler region. The gills start out whitish in color but turn brownish with age. The stem may be slightly swollen at the base, and is colored brownish in the lower portions, and nearly white in the upper portions, with a fibery appearance. Most of the time, a small ring will be present about two-thirds of the way up the stem, which has a noticeable upward flare. This species was historically named *Conocybe rugosa* until 2013.

DISTRIBUTION AND HABITAT: This species is widely distributed throughout most of North America; however, it is primarily found along the West Coast, from British Columbia to California, and in the Great Lakes and Appalachian regions. It is saprobic on woody debris on the ground, often in human-inhabited areas, and is primarily seen in the spring and summer months.

TOXIC AGENT(S): This species contains amatoxins, and should be considered deadly poisonous. Amatoxins are a group of peptides produced by several types of mushrooms. They inhibit protein synthesis, which leads to the death of the cells that are affected.

SIGNS AND SYMPTOMS OF POISONING: Exposure to toxins is through ingestion. Common symptoms include nausea, diarrhea, dizziness, and breathing difficulties. Liver and kidney damage are the end result, and can be fatal.

Rubroboletus pulcherrimus

RED-PORED BOLETE

**Rubroboletus from the Latin word for red (ruber) and
the Ancient Greek word for a type of edible mushroom (bolites),
pulcherrimus from the Latin word for "very beautiful."**

Boletaceae

DESCRIPTION: These can be large, robust-looking mushrooms, up to 20 cm in height, with caps up to 25 cm in width. Younger caps tend to have a rounded shape at first, eventually flattening out. The coloration of the cap's upper surface is usually an olive-red. The lower surface of the cap does not have gills, like most mushrooms, but has a flat surface completely covered by tiny pores, and is usually a pure red to reddish brown color. Upon handling, this pore surface will turn blue. The stems can be up to 10 cm wide at the base, but taper to 5 cm wide at the top. The stem color is usually some shade between yellow and brown. The upper portion of the stem usually is reticulate, looking as if a red-colored net is covering it.

DISTRIBUTION AND HABITAT: This species is native to coastal forests from California to British Columbia. It can be found growing as solitary individuals or in small groups, and it is mycorrhizal, associated with mixed conifer or hardwood species.

TOXIC AGENT(S): An alkaloid called muscarine is the toxin present in this species. Muscarine is a mimic of the neurotransmitter acetylcholine, and acts as a stimulant of the parasympathetic nervous system (PNS). The PNS is responsible for returning the body to a relaxed state after a stressful situation, as well as controlling processes such as digestion, urination, and sexual arousal.

SIGNS AND SYMPTOMS OF POISONING: Exposure to toxins is through ingestion. Symptoms usually appear within a couple of hours following ingestion, and include excessive salivation, lacrimation (tears), vomiting, diarrhea, abdominal pain, pupil constriction, and a decreased heart rate. Eventually, the body will enter circulatory shock due to low blood pressure and a decreased heart rate. Death can occur in as little as eight hours without treatment.

Sarcosphaera coronaria

PINK CROWN, VIOLET STAR CUP, VIOLET CROWN CUP

**Sarcosphaera from the Ancient Greek words
for flesh (sarx) and sphere (sphaira), *coronaria*
from the Latin word for crown (coronarius).**

Pezizaceae

DESCRIPTION: These develop in early to midspring as ball-shaped masses, primarily growing slightly below the soil surface. In early developmental stages, they appear similar to puffballs. As they develop, they emerge from the soil and split open, forming multiple ray-shaped folds on the upper surface of the fruiting body, and creating a cuplike structure from the original ball. The newly formed cups have a gray to violet lining and a white to cream exterior, making them relatively easy to distinguish from other cup fungi. The cups can be up to 20 cm across, and they sometimes form in clusters.

DISTRIBUTION AND HABITAT: *Sarcosphaera coronaria* is globally distributed. In North America, it is found in mycorrhizal associations with conifer species, and is an indicator of high-quality, well-preserved habitats for desirable edible species, like *Morchella*.

TOXIC AGENT(S): The toxicity of *Sarcosphaera coronaria* is something of a mystery. It was once listed as an edible species, with some reports of multiple instances of safe consumption followed by severe poisoning and, rarely, death. No specific fungal toxins have been identified, but more recent research has shown that nearly 1% of the dry weight of some *S. coronaria* specimens can be made of toxic arsenic compounds. *Sarcosphaera coronaria* has been shown to be an efficient bioaccumulator of arsenic from the soil. Arsenic can be acutely toxic, causing necrosis, inflammation of the stomach lining, and hepatic necrosis. It is also a known carcinogen.

SIGNS AND SYMPTOMS OF POISONING: All reported poisonings occurred after consuming boiled or fried fungal material. In acute cases, gastrointestinal distress, vomiting, and diarrhea may occur. Consuming lethal doses can result in cramping, convulsions, and pain, followed by numbness, tingling, and death due to respiratory failure. Continuous exposure to low doses may cause cancer.

Stachybotrys chartarum

TOXIC BLACK MOLD

Stachybotrys from the Greek words for progeny (stakhus) and cluster (botrus), *chartarum* from the Latin word for papers.

Stachybotryaceae

DESCRIPTION: *Stachybotrys chartarum* is a species of fungi that is naturally found in the soil, on plant debris. It is also the cause of the black mold that is sometimes found in human dwellings. In order to grow, the fungus requires darkness, a constant source of humidity, a substrate rich in cellulose, minimal competition from other microbes, and fluctuating temperatures. If present, it forms a greenish black, splotchy crust, usually at the site of constant moisture exposure. Identification can only be verified microscopically, as there are several other species that superficially look very similar.

DISTRIBUTION AND HABITAT: *Stachybotrys chartarum* has a cosmopolitan distribution and should be expected anywhere its favored growing conditions exist. Bathrooms and basements with cellulose-rich building materials and water problems, whether due to leaks or condensation, provide optimal growing conditions.

TOXIC AGENT(S): Fungal mycelia and spores contain terpenes called trichothecenes. Trichothecenes are readily absorbed through the skin and mucous membranes, and easily penetrate cell membranes. Once inside a cell, trichothecenes inhibit protein synthesis, which ultimately leads to cell death. Bone marrow and cells of the gastrointestinal tract are most susceptible to these toxins. Inhalation is the most likely route of exposure, as spores and mycelial fragments can become airborne when the mold is disturbed, such as when removal is attempted. Incidental ingestion is also a possibility.

SIGNS AND SYMPTOMS OF POISONING: Exposure to toxins is through inhalation or ingestion. Symptoms can be quite variable, depending on the route of exposure and dosage. "Sick building syndrome" has been attributed to black mold infestations, and is characterized by long-term incidences of sore throat, coughing or wheezing, malaise, headaches, nausea, and dermatitis. Normal levels of exposure are generally not considered deadly; however, heavily contaminated situations are potentially fatal, particularly in young children. Acute, high-level exposure to trichothecenes can cause severe pulmonary inflammation and hemorrhaging, which is especially dangerous for young children.

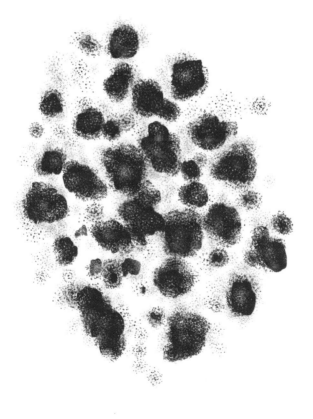

Xanthoparmelia chlorochroa

TUMBLEWEED LICHEN

**Xanthoparmelia from the Ancient Greek word
for yellow (xanthos) and the Latin word for shield (parma),
chlorochroa from the Ancient Greek word for green (khloros)
and the Greek word for color (chroia).**

Parmeliaceae

DESCRIPTION: These are free-living lichens, not attached to any substrate, and can get blown around like tumbleweeds. They are small and shrubby looking, with randomly twisted or contorted, leafy-looking "branches." The coloration is variable, and ranges from pale greenish gold to grayish green. Closer inspection will reveal that there is an upper and lower surface of the "branches," with the lower surface having more of a darker tan to brown color.

DISTRIBUTION AND HABITAT: This species is found primarily in dry areas adjacent to the Rocky Mountains, usually on sandy, open ground.

TOXIC AGENT(S): Unknown. Toxicity to humans has yet to be determined, but there are records of wild and domestic animals dying from eating these lichens.

SIGNS AND SYMPTOMS OF POISONING: Exposure to toxins is through ingestion. Wild elk that consumed these lichens became weak and listless, and also had bloody urine.

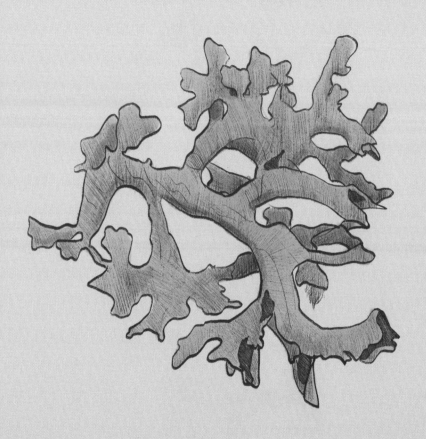

ABOUT THE AUTHOR

Dr. Kit Carlson earned her PhD in plant microbiology and pathology at the University of Missouri, and conducted her postdoctoral research at Virginia Tech, focused on molecular diagnostics of plant disease. Kit has been a botany professor for nearly two decades. During her tenure, she has served thousands of students and developed and instructed more than 15 different plant science courses. She and her students have conducted and published research on a wide range of topics, including plant disease, medicinal plants, ethnobotany, public land, science education, and more. She is also the coauthor of *Foraging: A Guide to Edible Wild Plants*, *The Book of Invasive Species*, and *How to Keep Your Plants Alive*.

ABOUT CIDER MILL PRESS BOOK PUBLISHERS

Good ideas ripen with time. From seed to harvest, Cider Mill Press brings fine reading, information, and entertainment together between the covers of its creatively crafted books. Our Cider Mill bears fruit twice a year, publishing a new crop of titles each spring and fall.

"Where Good Books Are Ready for Press"

501 Nelson Place
Nashville, Tennessee 37214

cidermillpress.com